LINE UPON LINE
PART 1

LINE UPON LINE
PART 1

Mrs F.L.Mortimer

Christian Focus Publications

© 2000 Christian Focus Publications

ISBN 1-85792-586-6

This edition published in 2000
by
Christian Focus Publications Ltd.
Geanies House, Fearn, Ross-shire,
IV20 1TW, Scotland, Great Britain.
(www.christianfocus.com ~ email:info@christianfocus.com)

Cover design by Owen Daily

Pinted and bound in Great Britain
by Cox and Wyman

PREFACE

Mrs Favell Lee Mortimer was born in 1802, the daughter of a London banker. She was religiously educated, and after her conversion at the age of 25, she threw herself with great enthusiasm into benevolent work. In particular, she was responsible for founding some parish schools on her father's estates, and was actively involved in their management.

At the age of 39 the author married Rev Thomas Mortimer, an Episcopal minister, but was widowed nine years later. After his death, she devoted her life to the care of the poor, and to writing books for the young. Her first great success was, "The Peep of Day," which passed through a great number of editions, and was translated into several languages. This was followed by further volumes, which included, "Line upon Line" in two parts. Her books made a lasting impact on the minds of the young in her day, and continue to influence generations long after her death in 1878.

In this edition of "Line Upon Line Part 1", every effort has been made to maintain as much of the original text as possible. It has been edited and adapted out of a desire to make it accessible to the contemporary reader whilst retaining the biblical accuracy and the author's ability to communicate with children.

Particular note should be taken of the new 'Suggestions for Study' which have been added to the start of each section and which include an activity which will involve the child in the next group of devotions.

Our hope is that this volume will be as much of a blessing in teaching today's generation as it was to previous ones.

Family Devotional Guide to the Bible

INTRODUCTION TO THE SERIES

The Family Devotional Guide to the Bible is made up of a series of six books which are excellent tools to use during your family devotional and worship times.

Although each book can be used on its own, the author's original intent was that they be used consecutively so that, starting with The Peep of Day, you and your children can go through the stories from the Bible together and discover the valuable lessons that can be learnt from them.

Using this series, you can progress from the story of Creation right through the Old Testament to the New Testament and the life, death and resurrection of the Lord Jesus Christ, the adventures and lessons of the Apostles and the early Christian Church.

All six books are an excellent family resource.

Family Devotional Guide to the Bible

BOOKS IN THE SERIES

1. The Peep of Day:
Lessons from both Old and New Testaments.

2. Line Upon Line I:
Lessons from Genesis, Exodus, Numbers and Joshua.

3. Line Upon Line II:
Lessons from 1st and 2nd Samuel, 1st and 2nd Kings, Daniel and Ezra.

4. Precept Upon Precept:
Lessons from the New Testament about the life, death and ressurection of Jesus Christ.

5. More About Jesus:
Further lessons from the New Testament about the life, death and ressurection of Jesus Christ.

6. Lines Left Out
Further Old Testament lessons not dealt with in The Peep of Day or Line Upon Line I and II.

USER'S INTRODUCTION

The aim of this book is to lead children to understand and to delight in the Scriptures.

If adults can meet with difficulties in the biblical text which commentaries will help them to overcome, children will obviously come across many more, some of which this book may help to clear up. Obviously the direction and teaching of a loving parent is the greatest help any child can have in understanding the Bible and its teaching, but this book and others in the series, will re-inforce that teaching and where parental guidance is not available this book will in some way help to fill that gap.

You should take particular note of the newly created 'Suggestions for Study' which have been added to the start of each section and which include an activity to involve your child in the next group of devotions.

Each chapter also contains a memory verse that relates in some way to the content of the chapter. Use these to encourage your child to commit these verses to memory as part of your study of the Bible.

In addition you will notice small numbers contained in the text of the chapters. These relate to notes provided at the end of each lesson, which you can use to encourage your child to get to know their way round their Bible by finding and reading the passages listed.

CONTENTS

SECTION 1
GENESIS

SECTION 2
EXODUS

SECTION 3
NUMBERS

SECTION 4
JOSHUA

SECTION 1

GENESIS

Introduction

The word 'genesis' means 'beginning' and as we look at this first book of the Bible, we learn about how everything came into being. God created all things good, and then he made man and woman to enjoy his creation and to look after it. What a disappointment, then, to discover that man turned away from God and did what was wrong.

Genesis explains that after the first people had chosen to disobey God they became selfish and evil and their behaviour brought pain and death to the human race. And then, there is a flash of hope, as we learn that God had an incredible plan to rescue us from the suffering we brought upon ourselves. It was worked out as he chose particular people to carry out his purposes. We see the beginnings of a whole nation who are special to God. It is from among them that Jesus will come and make it possible for all people to turn back to God.

Some Suggestions for Study

Genesis is about new beginnings and hope. As each lesson begins, think of some new things happening in your life. Maybe you have a new home or friends, new baby brother or sister, new class or term, or new things in town, like a sports centre, or shops. Think about the excitement, hope or fear these things might bring. Talk about how we might see Jesus at work in these new beginnings, and ask him to help you if you are struggling with them.

CHAPTER 1*
THE CREATION
Gen. 1.

I know that you have heard that God made the world. Could a man have made the world? No; a man could not make such a world as this.

Men can make some things, such as boxes and baskets. Perhaps you know a man who can make a box. Suppose you were to shut him up in a room, which was quite empty and you were to say to him, "You shall come out when you have made a box," would the man ever come out? No; never. A man could not make a box except he had something to make it of. He must have some wood, or some tin, or some pasteboard, or some other thing. But God had nothing to make the world of. He only spoke and it was made.[1]

Making things of nothing is called "creating". No one can create anything but God.[2]

Do you know why God is called the Creator? It is because he created all things. There is only one Creator. Angels cannot create things, nor can men. They could not create one drop of water, or one little fly.

You know that God was six days in creating the world. I will tell you what he did on each day.

Day 1

On the first day God said "Let there be light," and there was light.

Day 2

On the second day God spoke again and there was water

very high: that water is called the clouds. There was also water very low. There was nothing but water to be seen; God filled every place with air but you know the air cannot be seen.

Day 3

On the third day God spoke and the dry land appeared from under the water and the water ran down into one deep place that God had prepared.[3] God called the dry land Earth and he called the water Seas. We walk upon the dry land. We cannot walk upon the sea. The sea is always rolling up and down but it can never come out of the great place where God has put it. God spoke and things grew out of the earth. Can you tell me what things grew out of the earth? Grass and corn and trees and flowers.

Day 4

On the fourth day God spoke and the sun, moon and stars were made. God ordered the sun to come every morning and to go away in the evening[4] because God did not choose that it should be always light. It is best that it should be dark at night, when we are asleep. But God lets the moon shine in the night and the stars also; so that if we go out in the night we have a little light. There are more stars than we can count.

Day 5

On the fifth day God began to make things that are alive. He spoke and the water was filled with fishes and birds flew in the air and perched upon the trees.

Day 6

On the sixth day God spoke and the animals came out of the earth; lions, sheep, cows, horses and all kinds of animals, came out of the earth, as well as all kinds of creeping things, such as bees, ants and worms, which creep upon the earth.

At last God made a man. God said, "Let us make man in our own likeness."[5]

To whom did God speak? To his Son, the Lord Jesus Christ; his Son was with him when he made the world. God made man's body of the dust and then breathed into him. The man had a soul, as well as a body. So the man could think of God. Afterwards God made the woman out of a piece of flesh and bone from the man's side, as you have heard before.

God gave all the other creatures to Adam and Eve. He blessed them and put them into the Garden of Eden and commanded Adam to take care of the garden.

When God had finished all his works he saw that they were very good. He was pleased with the things he had made. They were all very beautiful. The light was glorious; the air was good; the earth was lovely, clothed in green; the sun and moon shone bright in the heavens; the birds and animals and all the living creatures were good and happy and Adam and Eve were the best of all because they could think of God and praise him.

Day 7

You know there are seven days in the week. Now, on the seventh day God did not make anything but he rested from all his works. He called the seventh day his own day, because he rested on it. This is the reason people rest on the seventh day and call it the Lord's day. It is the Sabbath day. It is the day for praising God.[6]

None of the creatures that God had made in the six days could praise him with their tongues, except Adam and Eve. Angels in heaven and men upon the earth can praise God . My children, do you ever praise God? You have learned hymns in his praise.

Does God like to hear you praise him? Yes; when you think of him while you are praising him. Angels always praise God with their hearts, and so should we. Let us now count the things that God made on each day:

First day: light.
Second day: air and clouds.
Third day: earth and sea and the things that grow.
Fourth day: sun, moon and stars.
Fifth day: fish and birds.
Sixth day: animals,creeping things and Man.
Seventh day: nothing - God rested.

Questions for Chapter 1

Why is God called the Creator?
Can men or angels create things?
What did God create on the first day?
On the second day?
On the third day?
On the fourth day?
On the fifth day?
On the sixth day?
What was the last thing God made?
What did God do on the seventh day?
Which of the creatures can praise God?

Scripture Verse

How long was God in making the world.
'For in six days the Lord made heaven and earth, the sea and all that in them is and rested the seventh day...' - (Exod. 20:11).

Notes for Chapter 1

* The Teacher will generally find the proof of every statement either in the chapters of the Bible referred to at the beginning of each chapter in this book, or in the notes affixed but in the opening of this work the proofs are often withheld, because they have already been given in those parts of "The Peep of Day" in which the same subjects are treated.

[1.] Heb. 11:3.   [2.] Rev. 4:11.   [3.] Job. 38:8,10.
[4.] Ps. 104:19.   [5.] John 1:1,3.   [6.] Ps. 42:4.

* * * * * * * * * *

CHAPTER 2
THE SIN OF ADAM
Gen. 3.

You remember that God put Adam and Eve in a pretty garden. There they lived very happily. They never quarrelled with each other; they were never sick nor in pain. Adam worked in the garden but not so hard as to tire himself. His work was quite pleasant for it was never too hot nor too cold in that garden and there were no weeds or thistles growing out of the ground.

You know there was one tree of which Adam was not to eat. The name of the tree was, "The tree of knowledge of good and evil".

God had said that if Adam ate of it he should die. Adam and Eve were allowed to eat of all the other trees in the garden.

Do you not think that they had fruit enough without eating of the tree of knowledge of good and evil? They did not wish to eat from it, as God had told them not to. They loved God. He was their friend and used to walk and talk with them in the garden. Now you shall hear how Adam and Eve grew wicked.

You know that there are many wicked angels; one of them is called "Satan," and he is the prince of the wicked angels.

Satan knew that if Adam and Eve grew wicked they would die and go to hell. Satan hated them and wanted to make them unhappy; so he thought, "I will try and persuade them to eat that fruit which God has told them not to eat." So Satan put on the body of a serpent[1] and came into the garden.

He saw Eve. Pretending to be kind he said to her, "Why do you not eat of the fruit?"

But she said, "God has told us not to eat of the fruit and that if we do we shall die."

But the serpent said, "No; you shall not die: but this fruit will make you wise like God."

The woman was afraid to eat but she looked and thought the fruit nice; she looked again and thought it pretty;[2] and she thought, "I should like to be wise." So she took the fruit and gave some to Adam.

Sad was that hour! No more happy days for Adam and Eve. They had grown naughty; they knew they had done wrong; they were afraid of God. Soon they heard his voice in the garden; they went and hid themselves among the thick trees. They wished they had some clothes to cover them but they had only some leaves that they sewed together.

God called Adam and said, "Where are you?"

Then Adam said, "I was afraid, because I was naked and I hid myself."

Then God said, "Who told you that you were naked? Have you eaten of that tree?"

Then Adam said, "The woman you gave to be with me, she gave me the fruit and I ate."

God said to the woman, "What is this that you have done?"

And she said, "The serpent deceived me and I ate."

God was angry with them all but most of all with the serpent. God cursed him and said, "You will always crawl on the ground and eat dust."

Then God said to the woman, "You shall often be sick and Adam shall be your master and you must obey him."

And God said to Adam, "You shall work hard and dig the ground: thorns and thistles will grow: you will have bread to eat but you will be obliged to work so hard that drops of sweat shall often be on your forehead; you will be sad while you live and at last you will die; your body was made of dust and it will turn into dust again."

What great punishments these were! How sad Adam and Eve must have felt when they heard them! But this was not all; they were not allowed to stay in the pretty garden. God drove them out and God would not let them come into the garden again; so he set an angel with a fiery sword to guard it. Yet, God showed his pity by giving them clothes made of skins of animals. They had tried to make clothes of the leaves of the trees but God gave them better ones.

Where do you think the souls of Adam and Eve must go when their bodies are dead? To Satan? That was what Satan hoped. But God had determined to send down his blessed Son to save Adam and Eve and their children, from hell and Jesus had promised to come.

Adam and Eve knew that a child would one day be born, who would save people from going to hell.[3] So they had some comfort in their hearts when they went out of the garden.

It was a long time before Jesus did become a little child and did come into this world but at last he came and died upon the cross.

My little children, wasn't it very kind of the Father to send his loved Son to die for us? Don't you think we should love him very much?

Questions for Chapter 2

Of what tree was Adam forbidden to eat?

Who asked Eve to eat from it?

Why did Eve eat some?

To whom did Eve give some of the fruit?

What punishment did God give to the serpent?

What punishment did he give to Eve?

What punishment did he give to Adam?

Why didn't God allow Adam and Eve to stay in the Garden of Eden?

What had the Son of God promised to his Father?

Scripture Verse

Who are the devil's children?

'He that committeth sin is of the devil; for the devil sinneth from the beginning...' - (1 John 3:8).

Notes for Chapter 2

[1] Rev. 12:9.   [2] Gen. 3:6.   [3] Gen. 3:15.

* * * * * * * * * *

CHAPTER 3
CAIN AND ABEL
Gen. 4.

After Adam and Eve were driven out of the garden, they had two children called Cain and Abel.

Cain was wicked like Satan but Abel was good; for though his heart was naughty God put his Holy Spirit in it, so that he loved God. Abel was sorry for his sins and asked God to forgive him;[1] and God did forgive him.

Cain and Abel were obliged to work hard, like Adam their

father. Cain farmed the ground, planting trees and reaping corn. Abel took care of the sheep. He was a shepherd.

Now I will tell you how Cain and Abel's attitude to God.

God did not walk and talk with people then, as he had done in the garden but he did speak sometimes and he allowed people to pray to him. You know that Jesus had promised to die for Adam and his children and that was the reason that God was so kind to them.

God wanted them always to remember that Jesus had promised to die for them; so he taught them a way of keeping it in their mind.

He told them to heap up stones (this heap was called an altar) and then to put some wood on the altar; then to take a lamb, or a kid, and to bind it with a rope to the altar; then to take a knife and to kill the lamb and finally, to burn it on the altar. Doing this was called "offering a sacrifice."

When people did this, God wanted them to think how he would one day let his Son die for their sins.[2] When Jesus was nailed to the cross, he was like a lamb tied to the altar.[3]

Abel brought lambs and offered them up to God and Abel thought of God's promise, so God was pleased with Abel and with his sacrifice. But Cain did not obey God, he brought some fruit instead of a lamb and so God was angry with Cain and did not like his sacrifice.

Then Cain was very angry and hated Abel, because he was good and because God loved him best. Cain was envious of Abel. Then God spoke to Cain and said, "Why are you angry? If you will love and serve me, I shall be pleased with you but if not, you shall be punished."

Still Cain went on in his wicked ways. Now, hear what he did; one day he was talking with Abel in a field, when he suddenly killed him.

Abel's blood was shed upon the ground; Abel was the first man that ever died. So Cain began by hating Abel and ended by killing him, though he was his brother.

Soon Cain heard the voice of God calling him. God said, "Where is your brother Abel?"

"I do not know," answered Cain, "am I my brother's keeper?"

But God said, "I have seen your brother's blood upon the ground and you are cursed. You shall leave your father and your mother and go far away."

Then Cain said to God, "My punishment is greater than I can bear. O do not let me be killed!"

God said, "You shall not be killed but you shall go to a place far away.[4]

So Cain went and lived far away and built houses for himself and his children. They lived in wickedness; they were the children of the devil and didn't care about God.

So Adam and Eve lost both their sons in one day; for Cain went away and Abel died. How they must have wept as they put Abel in the ground! But they must have wept still more to think that Cain was so wicked.

Why did they eat the fruit when Satan encouraged them to? If they had not eaten the fruit they would never have been unhappy; Cain would not have been wicked and Abel would not have died. But God had pity on Adam and Eve and gave them another son. He was made good by God's Spirit and was called Seth. The children of Seth feared God and God loved them and called them his children.

Questions for Chapter 3

What were the names of the two elder sons of Adam and Eve?
Had Adam's children naughty hearts?

How did God make Abel good?

What work did Cain do?

What work did Abel do?

How did people offer sacrifices?

What was the heap of stones called, on which the lamb or kid was burnt?

Why did God desire people to offer sacrifices?

Why did God like Abel's sacrifice better than Cain's?

Why did Cain kill Abel?

How did Cain answer God when he asked him where Abel was?

What punishment did God give to Cain?

What was the name of Adam's youngest son?

Scripture Verse

About Cain.

'...Cain, who was of that wicked one and slew his brother.' - (1 John 3:12).

Notes for Chapter 3

[1] Rom. 3:23. Heb. 11:2.   [2] Heb. 11:4.   [3] John 1:29.

[4] Commentators say that Cain did not become a wanderer but an outcast.

* * * * * * * * * *

CHAPTER 4
THE FLOOD
Gen. 6; 7; 8; 9.

Cain and Seth had a many children.

At last Adam and Eve died, as did Cain and Seth but still there were a lots of people in the world. Were the people good or wicked?

At first some were good but eventually they all grew wicked, except one man; his name was Noah.[1] The Spirit of God was in his heart and he loved God.

God was very angry with the wicked people and he decided to punish them.

God said to Noah, "I shall make it rain so much that all people will be drowned, except you, your wife and your children." Then God told Noah to make a enormous ark. What is an ark? It is like a boat or a ship. Noah made a very big ark, which would float upon the top of the water when God drowned the wicked people.

Noah made the ark of wood. Noah cut down many trees and cut boards and fastened them together. He made one door in the ark and one little window at the top.

Noah told the people that God was going to flood the world and advised them to stop their wickedness.

But they didn't care. They continued eating and drinking and ignoring God.[2]

God did not desire that all the animals, birds and insects would be drowned; so he directed Noah to get some birds, animals and insects of every sort and to bring them into the ark. God could make all these animals go quietly into the ark. Noah put corn and fruit and grass into the ark for them to eat when they were in the ark.

So Noah got some birds of every kind; some doves, some ravens, some eagles, some sparrows, some larks, some goldfinches and many others and they flew in at the window. Noah got some animals of every kind; some sheep, some horses, some dogs and he got some insects of every kind; some butterflies, some ants, some bees.

All these went into the ark because God made them gentle and obedient. Then Noah himself went in with his wife, his three sons and their wives. How many people were there in the ark? Eight people. But Noah did not shut the door: God shut the door and Noah knew that he must not open it till God told him to.

Then it began to rain. It rained all day and night. What did the wicked people think now? How they must have wished that they had listened to Noah! If they climbed trees, the water would soon reach the tops; if they went up high mountains, as high as the clouds, the water rose as high as they were because it rained forty days and forty nights. All animals and birds, men and children died, except those that were in the ark.

At last nothing was to be seen but water and the ark floating upon it. How long did Noah live in the ark? Almost one whole year.

A long time after it had stopped raining, Noah wanted to know whether the waters were dried up. He went among his birds and he chose a raven and let it out of the window. A raven is a fierce bird. It did not like the ark; though there were no trees to be seen, nothing but water, yet the raven would not go back to Noah but went on flying night and day over the water.

When Noah saw that the raven did not come back, he chose another bird - a dove. A dove is a very gentle bird. Noah put it out of the window and when it saw nothing but water, the dove came back to the ark. Noah knew when his bird had come back (perhaps it pecked at the window) and he put out his hand and brought it in.

Noah waited seven days, then Noah sent the dove out again. This time the dove saw some trees; yet the dove did not stay but plucked off a leaf with its beak and came back to Noah. Noah must have loved his good little dove. Noah waited seven days more and then he sent the dove out again and this time it did not come back. Now Noah knew that the earth was dry but he waited in the ark till God told him to go out.

At last, God said, "Go out of the ark, you and your wife, your three sons and their three wives and the birds and the animals and all the insects."

When the door was open, the creatures came out. How glad the sheep must have been to lie down again upon the soft grass and the goats to climb the high hills!

When the window was open the birds flew out. How glad they must have been to perch in the trees again!

Noah saw the green hills and fields again but where were all the wicked people? He would never see their faces again.

Noah remembered God's goodness in saving him from being drowned. He made a heap of stones for an altar, took some animals and birds and offered a sacrifice to God. God was pleased with this sacrifice.

Then God made a very kind promise to Noah. He said, "I will never drown the world again. When it rains, do not think there will be a flood. Look up in the sky after the rain and you will see a rainbow. That shall be a sign that I remember my promise."

Have you seen a rainbow? Isn't it big! What beautiful colours it has! It reminds us of God's kind promise not to drown the world again.

You know why God made this kind promise. It was because the Lord Jesus would one day die for people's sins.

At last Jesus did come down and die and one day he will come again and then he will judge the world. I hope we shall then be saved, as Noah was but if God should find us caring only about eating and drinking and playing and not trying to please him, we shall be judged too.[3]

Questions for Chapter 4

Why did God decide to drown the world?

How was Noah saved?

Did God let the wicked people know that the world was about to be drowned?

What birds did Noah send out of the ark to see whether the earth was dry?

What promise did God make to Noah?

What should the rainbow remind us of when we see it?

Scripture Verse

About the flood.

'[God] spared not the world but saved Noah, the eighth person, a preacher of righteousness, bringing in the flood upon the world of the ungodly.' - (2 Pet. 2:5).

Notes for Chapter 4

1. 2 Pet. 2:5.   2. Luke 17:27. 3. Luke 21:34.

* * * * * * * * * *

CHAPTER 5
ABRAHAM AND THE PROMISED LAND
Gen. 12:1-9.

Noah's sons had many children and in turn *they* had many children. Eventually there was many people in the world. Were these people good or bad? They were bad. They did one very wicked thing. They cut down trees and made the wood into little images like dolls; then stuck them up and kneeled down and prayed to the images and said, "These images are our gods. They made us and they gave us food to eat." These images were called idols.

Most of the people in the world worshipped idols instead of the true God. Sometimes the idols were made of wood, sometimes of stone, or silver, or gold.

How glad I am that your mothers did not teach you to pray to idols! When you began to speak they told you about the true God and taught you to pray to him.

God looked down from heaven and saw the people worshipping idols and he was very angry.[1] But he did not kill them all, because Jesus had said he would die for the sins of men.[2]

God said, "I will choose one man and teach him to love me and to be my servant."[3] Now there was a man called Abraham. His father and his friends worshipped idols. God said to Abraham, "Leave your own home and your own friends and go to a country which I will show you and I will bless you and take care of you."

Abraham did not know where God would tell him to go,[4] yet he went because God told him to go. Abraham was obedient.

Abraham had a wife, called Sarah, whom he loved very much. Sarah went with him. Abraham took some sheep and cows and donkeys with him and some servants, who drove and fed them.

But where could Abraham sleep at night? There were very few houses to be seen; only fields and trees. Abraham slept in a tent. He made the tent with long sticks and covered it over with animal skins.

Abraham could move his tent from place to place; for he had to travel a many miles over high hills and wide rivers. At last he came to a beautiful country, full of trees and flowers, grass and corn. This was the place that God chose for Abraham to live in. It was called Canaan.

Abraham still lived in a tent. Sometimes he made a heap of

stones called an altar and offered animal sacrifices to God. Abraham never worshipped idols but all the people in Canaan did.

God often spoke to Abraham and said, "I will bless you and take care of you and no one will hurt you." God was pleased that Abraham had left his own home when he had told him to and so God called him his friend.[5]

I hope that you will be like Abraham and that you will obey what God says in the Bible. God has not told you to leave your home but he has told you to be good and gentle, to speak the truth and to love him and he has promised to take you to heaven. If you obey God he will call you his friend.[6] How good it is to be God's friend.

Questions for Chapter 5

Whom did most of the people in the world pray to?
Who did God choose to be his servant and friend?
What was the name of Abraham's wife?
What did Abraham live in when he travelled?
To what land did God take Abraham?
What kind of people lived in Canaan?
Why was God pleased with Abraham?
What did God call him?
Can you be God's friend?

Scripture Verse

Who are God's friends.
'Ye are my friends, if ye do whatsoever I command you.' - (John 15:14).

Notes for Chapter 5

[1] Rom. 1:18,20,21.   [2] Isa. 49:6; Acts 17:30.

3. Isa. 41:2; Josh. 24:2; Neh. 9:7.
4. Heb. 11:8.   5. Jam. 2:23.   6. John 15:14.

* * * * * * * * * *

CHAPTER 6
ABRAHAM AND THE PROMISED CHILD
Gen. 15; 18:1-22; 21:1-6.

Abraham and Sarah lived in a tent in the land of Canaan. They had no children. Abraham was a very old man and Sarah was a very old woman. They were both much older than your grandfather and grandmother. Abraham was almost one hundred years old and Sarah was almost ninety.

One night God said to Abraham, "Come out of your tent and look up at the sky. What do you see?"

The sky was full of stars, more than could be counted. And God said, "You shall have a many, many grand-children and great-grand-children and they shall have more children, till there are as many children as there are stars in the sky. They shall live in the land of Canaan and the wicked people shall be driven out of it."

Now Abraham had not even *one* child; yet he believed that God would do as he had promised. It was right of Abraham to believe all that God said because God always speaks the truth and keeps his word.

One day Abraham was sitting in his tent. It was about mid-day and very hot indeed. however, the tent was under a tree. Abraham looked up and he saw three men a short distance away. He ran to meet them and bowed down and said to one of the men, "My lord, please come and rest yourself. Let me bring a little water to wash your feet and a little bread for you to eat and then you can continue your journey." And the men said they would rest themselves.

Who do you think these men were? They were angels, though they looked like men. They had come from heaven with a message from God for Abraham. You know that God sends his angels with messages to men. Angels are often near us, though we cannot see them.

The angels sat outside the tent, under the shade of the tree. Sarah was in the tent and Abraham said to her, "Take some flour and make some cakes and bake them very quickly." Then Abraham ran to his cattle and took a fat calf and said to one of his servants, "Kill it and roast it quickly."

When it was ready, Abraham brought some butter, some milk, the cakes and the calf and laid out the meal under the tree. The three men began to eat and Abraham stood near by.

While they were eating, they said to Abraham, "Where is Sarah your wife?" And Abraham said, "She is in the tent." Then one of the men said, "Sarah will have a son."

Sarah heard what the angel said and could not believe that she would *really* have a child, now that she was so very old and so she laughed to herself.

The angel said, "Why did Sarah laugh? She will certainly have a son." Then Sarah said, "I did not laugh"; for she was afraid. But the angel said, "You did laugh."

Then the three men got up and went on a little further. Abraham walked a little way with them and then came back to his tent.

Do you think that God remembered his promise? The next year Sarah had a son. His name was Isaac. He was a good child and God loved him. Abraham and Sarah were very pleased with their little son.

So you see that God kept his promise. He had said that

Abraham and Sarah would have a son and so he gave them a
son. It was right of Abraham to believe God's promise. God,
too, was pleased with Abraham for believing what he said.[1]
Sarah did not believe at first but she believed afterwards,[2] and
so God was pleased with her, too.

You should believe all God's promises. What has God
promised? To give you the Holy Spirit, if you ask him. Do you
believe his promise? Then pray to God to give you the Spirit.
He will keep his promise and give his Spirit to you.

Questions for Chapter 6

How many grandchildren and great-grandchildren did God
promise to give to Abraham?
Why did three angels come to Abraham's tent?
How did Abraham treat them?
How soon did they say that Abraham and Sarah would have a
son?
Did Sarah believe at first?
Did God keep his promise?
What was the son's name?
Why was God pleased with Abraham?

Scripture Verse

How Abraham pleased God.
'And he [Abraham] believed in the Lord and he counted it to
him for righteousness.' - (Gen. 15:6).

Notes for Chapter 6

[1] Rom. 4:20-22.   [2] Heb. 11:11.

CHAPTER 7
ABRAHAM AND THE TRIAL OF LOVE
Gen. 22.

At last, Isaac grew up to be a man. He lived in a tent, as Abraham and Sarah did. All three of them loved God and loved each other very much. It was a happy little family.

Now you know that Abraham had a many possessions. He had cows and donkeys, sheep and goats, tents and servants, silver and gold. But he had one thing that he loved more than any of these. What was that? His son, his dear son, Isaac. He loved him more than anything else he had.

Yet there was one person whom Abraham loved even better still. Who was that? God. Why did Abraham love God more than anything else? Because God had given him all he had.

God said he would test Abraham, to see whether he loved him more than *anything* in the world; more even than he loved his son Isaac. You have heard how Abraham used to burn lambs upon altars. Now God said to Abraham, "Take your dear son Isaac and sacrifice him on an altar in a place that I will show you."

Wasn't this a very hard thing for Abraham to do? But Abraham wanted to do all God told him; because Abraham loved God so much. So Abraham cut down some wood to burn. He put the wood on a donkey and he told two of his servants and Isaac to come with him. He left Sarah in the tent at home. All four of them walked for three days until at last they saw a high hill in the distance. Abraham knew that was the place where he was to build the altar. So he said to his servants, "Stay down here with the donkey, while I and the boy go and worship God on the top of the hill." He took the wood off the donkey and tied it up for Isaac to carry. Then taking some fire in one hand and a knife in the other, Abraham took Isaac up the hill.

Isaac did not know that his father was going to offer him as a sacrifice. He thought that his father would offer a lamb. So he said, "Father." Abraham answered, "Here am I, my son." And Isaac said, "Here is the fire and wood but where is the lamb?" "My son," said Abraham, "God will find a lamb". Abraham did not tell Isaac that he was to be the lamb.

At last they came to the top of the hill. Then Abraham took stones and built an altar. Then he took the wood off Isaac's back and laid it on the altar. Now the time was come when Isaac must know who was to be the lamb. The rope that had bound the wood was tied around the Isaac's feet and hands. He was then laid upon the wood on the altar, like a lamb.

Abraham took the knife and lifted up his hand to kill Isaac when he heard a voice calling, "Abraham, Abraham!" It was an angel speaking from heaven. The angel said, "Do not kill your son, or hurt him at all for now God knows that you love him because you have given him your only son."

How glad Abraham was to untie the rope that bound Isaac and to find that he didn't have to kill him!

Abraham saw a ram, caught by it's horns, in the bushes. He went and took it and offered it up as a sacrifice instead of Isaac. Abraham thanked God very much for having given him back his son and the angel called to him out of heaven again and said, "God is very pleased with you for having given up your son and God will bless you and all your children, grandchildren and their children and one of your children's children will make all people happy."[1]

Who did the angel mean? He meant Jesus would one day be a child and make people happy and take them to heaven. A very, very long time afterwards, you know, that Mary had a child who was the Son of God.

When the angel had finished speaking Abraham and Isaac went down the hill together. There was no wood on Isaac's back. Abraham was very glad. They found the servants where they had left them with the donkey. Then together they all went back to Sarah.

Are you quite sure that Abraham loved God? How do you *know* that he did? Because he obeyed God and was ready to kill his son when God told him.[2] Should you love God better than everything as well? Yes, you should love God best. And why? Because God gave you everything.

You love your father and mother very much but you should love God better still. You should love God much even more than playing, or your possessions, or good food and sweets. Now, if you love God this much you will do what he tells you. You will not tell lies because God tells you not to; you will not loose your temper and call people names: but you will try and please God. Then you will be like Abraham.

Questions for Chapter 7

Why did God tell Abraham to offer up his son as a sacrifice?
Was Abraham going to do what God told him?
What did Isaac say to his father as he walked up the hill?
What did Abraham do when he was on the top of the hill?
How was Abraham stopped from killing Isaac?
Why should we to love God more than everyone else?

Scripture Verse

Who loves God.
'He that hath my commandments and keepeth them, he it is that loveth me...' - (John 14:21).

Notes for Chapter 7

[1.] Gal. 3:16.   2. John 14:21.

* * * * * * * * * *

CHAPTER 8
JACOB AND THE HEAVENLY DREAM
Gen. 23; 25; 27; 28.

Abraham and Sarah were very, very old. Eventually, Sarah died and Abraham wished to bury her but he did not have a piece of ground in Canaan to bury her in. So he gave some of his silver to the people in Canaan and bought a field. The field was full of trees and there was a cave in it. Abraham took the sarah's body and put it in the cave. Eventually, Abraham died and Isaac his son buried him in the same cave where Sarah lay.

Abraham will rise again out of that cave on the last day.

Abraham's spirit is not dead; it is with God now,[1] and on the last day his body will live too and you will see him. If you love God as Abraham did you will sit down with Abraham in heaven.[2]

Isaac married a good woman named Rebekah. She lived in the tent where Sarah used to live.

Isaac and Rebekah had two sons. They were called Esau and Jacob. They were twins but not identical - they were quite unlike each other. Their faces were unlike and their hearts were unlike. Esau was wicked from a child but Jacob was good and loved God. When Esau was a man he became a hunter. He had a bow and arrows and used to go in the woods and shoot birds and stags. He would bring them home and prepare them for dinner and gave some of his nice meat to his father Isaac.

It was not wrong for Esau to hunt and to cook the meat but

his heart was wicked. He did not care for God and he loved meat and drink more than God.[3]

Jacob was a shepherd. He stayed at home near his tent with his father and mother and his sheep and goats. He loved God and often prayed to God.

I am sorry to tell you that Isaac loved wicked Esau more than he loved good Jacob. Shall I tell you why? Because Esau brought him nice meat. That was a very bad reason for loving him the most.

However, Rebekah loved Jacob and God loved Jacob and God did not love Esau.[4] Do you think that Esau and Jacob loved one another?

They did not; Jacob was sometimes unkind to Esau and so Esau hated Jacob and wanted to kill him. One day Esau said, "My father will soon die and then I will kill my brother Jacob."

Rebekah heard that Esau planned to kill Jacob some day, so she was frightened and called Jacob and said to him, "Your brother Esau wants to kill you. This is what you must do; go to your uncle, who lives far away, and stay with him. Soon Esau will calm down; then I will send for you to come home."

Jacob did as his mother advised. Then Jacob with only took a stick in his hand[5], without servants, sheep or goats - not even a donkey to ride upon, set out on his journey. He felt very sad. He was a poor traveller and he was going to a distant country which he had never seen.

Wouldn't you feel very sad if you were to leave your father and mother and to go alone into a country far away?

He had no tent or house to sleep in on the way, so when night came he took some stones for a pillow and lay down to sleep on the ground. There were bears and wolves in that country but God took care of him. God knew how sad he was and God made him dream an amazing dream.

In his sleep Jacob saw lots of steps reaching up to the sky. On the steps were beautiful angels; some going up and some coming down. At the top he saw God himself. Then Jacob heard a voice and God spoke to him and said, "I am the God of Abraham and Isaac and I will take care of you wherever you go. I will bring you home again and your children will live in this land of Canaan, where you are sleeping."

Then Jacob woke up with a gladness in his heart. He knew that God and his angels were watching over him. He never wanted to forget the place where he had this wonderful dream; so he took the stones, which had been his pillow and made them into a pile. "Now," he thought, "I shall be able to find the place, when God lets me come back to Canaan, as he has promised." He could not offer a sacrifice upon the stones, because he had no lambs but he poured some oil on them,[6] and he prayed to the Lord and said, "Since God will take care of me and give me bread to eat and clothes to wear and bring me home again, he shall be my God and this stone shall be God's house."

Jacob felt sure that God would take care of him and bring him home again because he had promised that he would.

God takes care of you. He sends his angels down from heaven to watch over you, as they did over Jacob.

Questions for Chapter 8

Who buried Sarah?
Where was she buried?
Who was Isaac's wife?
What were the names of Isaac's children?
What were their jobs?
Did they love God?
Why did Jacob leave his house and go to a far away country?

What dream did he have as he slept on the ground?
When Jacob awoke, what did he do?
What did he say to God?

Scripture Verse

How safe the righteous are.
'For the eyes of the Lord are over the righteous and his ears are open unto their prayers...' - (1 Pet. 3:12).

Notes for Chapter 8

[1] Luke 20: 37,38   [2] Matt. 8:11. [3] Heb. 12:16.
[4] Rom. 9:13.   [5] Gen. 32:10. [6] Gen. 28:18.

* * * * * * * * * *

CHAPTER 9
JACOB AND THE LONG JOURNEY.
Gen. 29.

Jacob went on his journey. He travelled for many days and eventually came to a place where there was a great deal of grass. In that place there was a well and there was a great stone upon the top of the well. Lots of sheep were round the well and some men were with the sheep. These men were shepherds. There was very little water in that country where Jacob was. He must have been glad to see a well.

Jacob said to the shepherds, "Do you know a man called Laban?" (That was the name of Jacob's uncle.)

"Yes," said they, "we do."

Then Jacob said, "Is he well?"

The shepherds answered, "He is well and here is his daughter Rachel coming with the sheep."

Jacob was very glad to hear this because Rachel was

Jacob's cousin. He ran to her and kissed her and he sobbed and wept.

Why did Jacob cry?

I think he cried for joy because people sometimes cry for joy.

Jacob had not seen a friend for a long time and he was glad to see his cousin.

Rachel did not know who Jacob was, till he said, "I am your cousin and am come from far away."

Then Rachel ran and said to her father Laban, "My cousin Jacob has come; I found him sitting by a well."

Then Laban was glad and ran out to meet Jacob, kissed him and said, "You must come home to my house. I am your uncle."

Jacob told Laban that he would take care of his sheep; and so Jacob was Laban's servant. Jacob was a good shepherd and sat up to guard the sheep at night from lions and bears. He did not care about the heat by day or the cold by night.[1]

Laban had two daughters; one was called Leah and the other Rachel and Laban gave them to Jacob to be his wives. So Jacob had two wives. No one may have two wives *now* but *then* some persons had two wives, yet even then it was much better to have only one wife.

God gave Jacob lots of children. I will not tell you their names because they were so many. Jacob lived a long time in some tents with his wives and his children. At first he took care of Laban's sheep only. Eventually, Laban gave Jacob some sheep and goats of his own. Jacob had plenty of bread to eat and cloths to wear, as God had promised. God always keeps his promises.

But Jacob could not forget his father and mother and Canaan, where he had lived when he was a boy. He knew that

God had promised to give the Land of Canaan to Abraham's children and Isaac's children and to his own children,[2] and he wanted to live there again.

I will now write down the names of the good men who first lived in Canaan and I will write down the names of their wives.

Abraham   - Sarah.

   |

Isaac   - Rebekah.

   |

Jacob   - Leah and Rachel.

Questions for Chapter 9

Who was Rachel?

Where did Jacob first see her?

What was the name of Jacob's uncle?

What did Jacob do for Laban?

Who were Jacob's wives?

Did Jacob have any sheep and goats of his own?

Why did Jacob want to live in Canaan again?

Scripture Verse

How happy the righteous are.

'Blessed is every one that feareth the Lord; that walketh in his ways.' - (Ps.128:1).

CHAPTER 10
JACOB AND THE MEETING.
Gen. 31; 32; 33; 35:1-7.

Eventually, Jacob said to Laban, his uncle, "I have been your servant a long time and now I want to go home." But Laban would not let Jacob go away and he behaved very unkindly to Jacob. So Jacob wanted to go home even more.

Once, while Jacob was taking care of the sheep in the field, he fell asleep and had a dream. In his dream he heard God say to him, "Go home to your father and I will be with you."

When Jacob woke up he sent a servant to fetch Rachel and Leah. He said to them, "God has spoken to me in a dream and has told me to return home to my father."

Then Rachel and Leah said, "We will go with you."

Then Jacob packed up all his things - his tents, his clothes and all his belongings. He put his things on the backs of his camels and donkeys and placed his wives and his eleven children on camels. He told his servants to drive all his sheep, cows, goats and donkeys and camels. So they all set off.

Laban did not see Jacob go; for Jacob tents were not close to the place where Laban lived. Eventually, Laban heard that Jacob had gone. He was angry and went after Jacob. He begged Jacob to come back but Jacob wanted to go to Canaan.

Jacob was pleased to go back to Canaan but there was one thing that frightened him. He remembered that Esau had once said that he would kill him. Jacob was afraid that Esau might now come and kill him and his children.

Soon, Jacob heard that Esau was coming with four hundred men. Jacob now thought that Esau was really coming to kill him. So he began to pray to God and said, "O God, you have been very kind to me and given me lots of things, do not let Esau come and hurt me and kill my wives and my children. You promised to take care of me." God heard Jacob's prayer.

Jacob thought to himself, "I will send a present to show Esau that I wish to be kind to him." So he took lots of goats, sheep, cows, donkeys and camels and told his servants to drive them on ahead and to tell Esau that he had sent them as a present. Jacob spent all that night seeking God.

In the morning Jacob looked up and saw Esau coming with four hundred men. Jacob did not run away but went up to Esau. As he walked he stopped seven times and bowed down to the ground.

And what did Esau do?

He ran and put his arms round Jacob's neck and kissed him - they both wept. God had softened Esau's heart.

How glad Jacob was to find that his brother had become kind! Jacob had prayed to God to make him kind and God had answered his prayer.

Esau looked up and saw Rachel and Leah and the children and said, "Who are these?"

And Jacob said, "These are my children, that God has been so kind as to give me."

Then Rachel and Leah bowed themselves to the ground and their maids bowed and all the children bowed, even the youngest, who was quite small. He was Rachel's child and his name was Joseph.

Then Esau said to Jacob, "I have lots of sheep and cows and goats - why did you send them on before you?"

Jacob said, "They were a present for you."

Esau answered, "I have enough, my brother, keep what you have for yourself."

"Please, take my present," said Jacob, "for God has given

me a great deal." And Jacob begged Esau to take it, so much, that eventually, he took it.

Esau said to Jacob, "Let us take our journey together and I will go on first."

But Jacob said, "I cannot go as fast as you do because I have many children with me and young lambs and kids and if one day we were to drive them too fast, they would die." So Jacob would not go with Esau.

Then Esau went home to his own house, which was far away; for Esau did not live in Canaan. But Jacob stayed in the land of Canaan because he wanted to live there.

You see that God had let Jacob come back to Canaan, as he had promised. Jacob did not forget the dream I told you of. He went to that very place once more. He had made a heap of stones to mark the place so that he could find it again. There he built an altar and offered sacrifices to God, who had been so kind to him. God had given him food and clothes, as he had promised, and he had given him many more things besides; for God had given him wives and children and servants and cattle God had also made his brother kind to him and had let him come back to Canaan. Jacob loved God very much and he thanked him for his kindness.

Hasn't God been very kind to you? Tell me what things he has given you. Can you think of ten or twelve things he has given you? Food, clothes, etc. Sometimes people have been unkind to you and God has made them grow kind. you should really love God!

Questions for Chapter 10

Who told Jacob to go home to his father?

What was Jacob afraid of when he was on his way home?

What was it Jacob did when he was afraid?

How did Esau behave to Jacob when he met him?

Did Jacob ever go again to the place where he had seen the angels?

What kind things had God done for Jacob since he had been there?

Scripture Verse

Jacob's thanks to God for keeping his kind promises.
'I am not worthy of the least of all the mercies and of all the truth, which thou hast showed unto they servant...' - (Gen. 32:10).

* * * * * * * * * *

CHAPTER 11
JOSEPH AND THE PIT

Jacob saw his old father Isaac again and then Isaac died. Jacob and Esau buried him in that same cave where Abraham and Sarah had been put. They will all rise together on the last day; for Isaac wanted to live in the country that is better than Canaan, that is, in heaven.

Esau, you know, did not live in the land of Canaan but Jacob chose to live in Canaan, with his children and his cattle.

All the sons had grown up to be men while Benjamin was still a baby. Joseph was the next youngest to Benjamin. He was a big boy and the best of all the children. The ten elder sons were wicked men. They used to take care of the sheep and goats and when Joseph was with them they upset him by their wicked behaviour. They were also very unkind to him and always spoke harshly to him. Jacob loved Joseph the most which made the others envious. They hated him, because he was the favourite.

Jacob gave a beautiful present to his dear son. It was a very pretty coat made of many colours - yellow, blue, green, pink, red, purple and Joseph used to wear it. The brothers were very envious when they saw this coat.

It is Satan that makes people envious. We should pray to God to keep us from being envious. You will hear what wicked things these brothers did, because they were envious of dear, good Joseph.

One night Joseph had a very strange dream. He thought he was in a field of corn with all his brothers and that they were making up large bundles of corn, called sheaves. He thought that each of his brothers made a sheaf and that all his brothers' sheaves bowed down to his sheaf. Joseph thought this was a very strange dream and he told it to his brothers.

But when they heard it they were very angry and said, "We think you mean that we should bow down to you, though you are younger than we are!" And so they hated him more than they had done before.

Soon after Joseph had another strange dream. He thought he saw the sun, moon and eleven stars in the sky and that they bowed down to him. This dream was stranger than the other and he told it to his father, as well as to his brothers.

His father was surprised and said, "Will your mother and I and your brothers bow down to you?" Yet Jacob thought that God had sent the dream to Joseph and would make it come true but the brothers were more and more angry.

Now Joseph's brothers had lots of sheep and goats to take care of and there was not enough grass for them all near the tents. So they took their flocks far away to fresh pasture. Joseph stayed at home with his old father and Benjamin.

Eventually, Jacob wanted to know how his sons were; so he said to Joseph, "Go and see your brothers and come back and tell me how they are and how the flocks are."

Joseph was always ready to do what his father wanted, so he set out on his way. He took no donkey to ride and no servant. He didn't realise how long it would be before he would again see his father's face again.

Joseph went a long way but could not find his brothers. Eventually, a man saw him and said, "Who are you looking for?"

And Joseph answered, "I am looking for my brothers - can you tell me where they are feeding their flocks?"

The man told him which way they had gone.

Joseph went to great trouble to find his brothers.

Now the brothers saw Joseph coming at a distance. They knew that it was Joseph and said to each other, "Here this dreamer comes, let us kill him and throw him into a deep hole and tell our father that a lion or a bear has eaten him!"

So when Joseph came up to them, they seized hold of him. He came to them full of love and kindness but they looked angrily at him; he was like a lamb in the middle of lions and tigers. He was like the Lord Jesus when the wicked people seized him in the garden.

The brothers were going to kill him but one of the brothers, Reuben, said, "Do not kill him. Throw him into a pit." Reuben was a kinder than the rest and intended to take him out of the pit and bring him back to Jacob. The brothers agreed not to kill him. But first they took off his coat.

Oh, how he cried when he saw what they were going to do to him! He begged them to spare him and to let him return to his father! But they would not hear,[1] for their hearts were harder than stones.

They threw him into a deep, dark pit and there he lay, hungry, thirsty and weary, without one drop of water. How it must have upset Joseph to think that he would not return to his dear father and that his father perhaps would think that he was dead.

The wicked brothers didn't care about his groans but sat down and began to eat their dinner.

God saw them from his throne in heaven and was very displeased.

Questions for Chapter 11

How many sons did Jacob have?

Which son did Jacob love the most?

Why didn't Joseph's brothers love him?

What did Jacob give to Joseph?

What two dreams did Joseph have?

Why did these dreams make the brothers angry with Joseph?

Why did Jacob send Joseph to his brothers when they were keeping sheep?

Where did the brothers throw him?

Scripture Verse

What a wicked man thinks when he is doing wickedness.
'He hath said in his heart, God hath forgotten. He hideth his face. He will never see it.' - (Ps. 10:11).

Notes for Chapter 11

[1.] Gen. 42:21.

CHAPTER 12
JOSEPH THE SLAVE
Gen. 37:24 - 35.

While the brothers were eating their dinner, they looked up and saw some people coming along. As the people came nearer they saw camels and men riding on them. I will tell you who these men were.

They lived in a far away country and had been to some hills, where very good things grew, called spice and balm. They had harvested these things and had put them in large bundles on the backs of their camels. They were going to carry them to a country far away and sell them for money. This was their way of getting their living and it was a good way; yet they were wicked men, as you will see.

One of the brothers, called Judah, said, "Let us sell Joseph to those men. It would be better to sell him than to kill him because we will get some money if we sell him and it would be cruel to kill Joseph as he is our brother."

Yet, wasn't it very cruel to sell Joseph? Judah was not really kind. The other brothers said that they thought it was a good plan to sell Jospeh. So they called to the men and asked them if they would buy a young boy.

The men said "Yes." This was wicked.

"How much will you give us for him?" said the brothers.

"We will give you twenty pieces of silver," said the men.

Then Joseph's brothers pulled Joseph out of the pit. Perhaps he thought they were going to let him return to his father.

Ah! Poor Joseph! He soon found that his brothers were not going to be kind. The men and the camels were waiting outside the pit. The men paid the money to the brothers and then took Joseph and carried him away with them.

When Joseph was gone, the brothers said, "What shall we tell our father when he asks us where Joseph is? We will not say we have seen Joseph but we will say we have found his coat on the ground!"

Then the brothers killed one of their young goats and dipped the coat in the blood. "We will show our father this blood stained coat," said they. So they carried the coat home, covered with blood, and they also took the money they got for selling Joseph.

Do you think they were happy in their hearts? Oh, no! The wicked cannot be happy. God has written down their wickedness in his book and they should feel afraid.

Joseph was not so unhappy as they must have been for God was his friend.

Old Jacob had been thinking of his sons while they were gone. How glad he must have been when he heard the bleating of their sheep and knew they had come home! He must have looked to see whether Joseph was with them. But no - his sons came up to him. In their hands they held a blood stained coat. They showed it to Jacob and said, "We have found this; do you think it is your son's coat, or not?"

Jacob knew that coat and said, "It is my son's coat; a lion or a bear has eaten him up and has torn Joseph to pieces!"

How Jacob wept for his child! How sorry he was that he had sent him, alone, to seek his brothers! The wicked brothers tried to comfort Jacob and said, "Do not weep so much" but Jacob would not listen.

"No; I shall die and then I will be with Joseph. I never will be happy any more."

How sad it was to see this poor old man, leaning on his stick, his grey hair and his face full of sadness, while he thought that his dear boy had been eaten up by a lion or a bear! His little Benjamin was a comfort to him. Jacob would never let him go away, nor would he trust him with his brothers, though he did not know how wicked they had been. These brothers first envied Joseph, then they had sold him and then they had told a lie to hide their sin.

Children sometimes try to hide their faults by telling lies and so they make God angrier than he was before. Remember that God always sees you and that he hates liars and will not let them live with him in glory.

Questions for Chapter 12

Who passed by Joseph's brothers while they ate near the pit?
What did Judah advise the brothers to do with Joseph?
How much did they sell him for?
What did the brothers do with Joseph's coat?
Why did they dip it in blood?
What did Jacob think when he saw it?
How do wicked people try to hide their faults?

Scripture Verse

How God will punish liars.
'...and all liars, shall have their part in the lake which burneth with fire and brimstone...' - (Rev. 21:8).

* * * * * * * * * *

CHAPTER 13
JOSEPH THE PRISONER
Gen. 39.

The men who had brought Joseph, took him to a country far away. It was called Egypt. When they got to Egypt they tried to sell him, as if he had been a horse or a cow. In this country, where we live, no one sells people. In some countries people are sold and are called slaves. They are beaten and made to work very hard but are not paid any money for their labour.

Poor Joseph was sold as a slave. Don't you hope that a kind man bought him? Well, it was a kind man who bought him. There was a very rich man who knew the king and he bought Joseph to be his slave. His name was Potiphar. He took Joseph home with him. He did not send him to work in the fields but made him a servant in the house. So Joseph did not have very hard work to do.

Joseph tried to be a good servant. Though he longed to be with his father he did not waste the time in fretting but worked hard to please his master. When his master told him to do something he did it so well that his master was very pleased. It was God that made Joseph able to do his work so well and Joseph's master knew this.[1] I suppose that Joseph had told him; for his master did not know the true God but worshipped idols.

Potiphar liked him better every day. Eventually, his master said to Joseph, "I can trust you so well that I will put you in charge of the other servants when I am out. Take care of the house and all the things in it, the garden and the fields; for I can trust you."

So Joseph had the responsiblity of everything and all the other servants obeyed what he said. He could have done what he pleased when his master was out. But Joseph behaved the same as if his master were watching him; for he knew God was always watching him. There are many children who behave badly as soon as their parents go out of the room. Such children do not fear God.

Though Joseph was in charge of nice things to eat and beautiful things to wear he only took what his master allowed him to take. He was always busy - sometimes in the house and sometimes in the field. God made things grow well in the field and the work go well in the house. Potiphar concern himself with the work for he found that Joseph could manage everything for him.

So Joseph now had all he could wish for but he could not forget his father and his little baby brother Benjamin. As for his mother, Rachel, she had died some time before.

Now you shall hear what a sad thing happened to Joseph.

Potiphar had a very wicked wife. She wanted Joseph to be turned out of the house because Joseph had found out how bad she was.

This wicked woman said to Potiphar, "Your slave, Joseph, that you think is so good, is very wicked and when you are out he behaves very badly." Then she told Potiphar of bad things that she said Joseph had done.

Potiphar was so foolish as to believe her and he got angry and said, "Joseph shall be put into prison."

So some men took Joseph and brought him to the prison, which was in the house of the captain of the guard.

Were you ever in a prison? It is a dark place with few windows and bars of iron on the windows and locked gates.

Joseph was put into prison and his feet were hurt by great iron chains which were put around them.[2]

There were lots of men in the prison and most of them had done very bad things but Joseph had done nothing wrong. God still loved Joseph and he could make him happy even in a prison.

There was a man who kept the keys of the prison and took care of the prisoners. He was called the keeper of the prison. Sometimes keepers are very unkind but God put it into the keeper's heart to love Joseph. Joseph had an honest face and he behaved well obeying all the keeper said.

Eventually, the keeper took the chains off Joseph's feet and allowed him to walk about the prison and take care of the other prisoners. The keeper found that he could trust Joseph and that he managed things well. It was God who made Joseph do everything so well; for God was Joseph's friend and was always watching over him and comforting him.

Joseph hoped that God would some day let him out of prison.

Questions for Chapter 13

Where was Joseph taken by the men who bought him from his brothers?

To whom did they sell Joseph?

How did Potiphar treat Joseph?

Who spoke against Joseph to Potiphar?

How did Potiphar punish Joseph?

How did the keeper treat Joseph?

Scripture Verse

What the Lord promises to do for the righteous.
'...I will be with him in trouble; I will deliver him and honour him.' - (Ps. 91:15).

Notes for Chapter 13

[1] Gen. 39:3.   [2] Ps. 105:17,18.

CHAPTER 14
JOSEPH AND THE BUTLER AND THE BAKER.
Gen. 40.

The prison, you remember, was in the house of the captain of the guard. One day this captain brought two men to Joseph and said, "Take great care that these men do not get out of prison. I put then in charge of them." So you see this captain thought Joseph could be trusted; perhaps he had found out that Joseph was not so bad as he had once thought - still he did not let Joseph out of prison.

I will tell you who these men were that this captain brought to Joseph; they were the servants of the king of Egypt. The king of Egypt had lots of servants to wait on him. One of his servants used to bring him wine in a cup to drink. This servant was called his butler. Another man used to bake things for his table and bring them to the king. He was called the baker.

The butler and the baker had both offended the king; I do not know what they had done but they had made the king so angry that he had said they should be shut up in prison.

So the king said to the captain, "Put these men into prison."

Then the captain brought them to Joseph and told him to keep them safe. Joseph shut them up in a room together and gave them bread and water every day taking good care of them.

One morning, when Joseph came to see them, he observed that they looked very sad indeed. So Joseph said to them, "Why do you look so very sad?"

They answered, "We have each had a very strange dream to-night and we think our dreams have some meaning but we cannot find out what it is and there is nobody in the prison who can tell us."

Then Joseph said, "But my God knows all things. He could tell me the meaning. Tell me your dreams."

The butler told his dream first. He said, "I thought I saw a vine that grow grapes. It had three branches but no grapes. While I was looking I saw little buds and they turned into grapes which grew and ripened. I picked the grapes and squeezed them into a cup and made wine. Then I brought the cup to the king for him to drink as I used to do."

This was the butler's dream and God told Joseph what it meant.

"You saw three branches," said Joseph; "something will happen to you in three days. The king will send for you to be his butler again."

When the baker heard this positive meaning, he thought that his dream would be good too, so he began to tell it. The baker said, "I dreamt that I was carrying three white baskets on my head, one on the top of the other. In the baskets there was baked food and birds came and picked the food out of the top basket."

The baker thought that Joseph would say, "In three days you will be baker again to the king." But this dream had a sad meaning.

"Something will happen to you in three days," said Joseph. "The king will send for you and will hang you upon a tree and the birds will pick off the flesh from your bones."

So, while the butler was pleased with what Joseph had told him, the poor baker was very sorry, because he knew that he would die.

Joseph had one little favour to ask of the butler. You can guess what it was. "When you are with the king of Egypt," Joseph asked, "giving him his wine, will you tell him about me?

Tell him how I am shut up in prison and cannot get out. I once lived in a land far away but I was stolen away. Now I am shut up in this prison, though I have done nothing wicked to deserve it. Beg the king to let me out."

You see Joseph did not tell about his brothers' wickedness in selling him.

In three days the king sent some men to the prison to fetch the butler and the baker. It was the king's birthday and he had made a feast for his servants and he had thought of the butler and the baker and had said, "Let the butler come back to me and let the baker be hanged; I will not forgive him." So now both the butler and the baker knew that Joseph had told them the truth.

Did the butler remember Joseph when he was with the king? No! He forgot all about him. I suppose he was thinking of the fine things he saw, of eating and drinking, of money and clothes and forgot that poor Joseph was in a prison. The butler was unkind, worse than unkind - he was ungrateful. Joseph had been good to him, yet he was not kind in return. Therefore, I call him ungrateful. Many children are ungrateful to their parents, who were good to them when they were little; and all people are ungrateful to God who gave his Son to die for them.

Poor Joseph waited in vain. No one came to let him out of prison. One day passed, then another. Summer came and then winter but Joseph was still locked up. Yet God had not forgotten him. Why did God make him wait so long? So that he might learn to be patient. If God allows you to be sick for a long time it is to make you patient. You should think to yourself, "God will make me well when he thinks it best."

Questions for Chapter 14

What two men did the captain place under Joseph's care?
What made them look sad one morning when Joseph came in?
What was the butler's dream?
What did it mean?
What was the baker's dream?
What did it mean?
What was it Joseph asked the butler to do for him?
Did the butler remember Joseph?
What is it "to be ungrateful"?
Who begs for us in heaven?

Scripture Verse

The Lord likes men to be patient.
'The Lord is good unto them that wait for him, to the soul that
seeketh him.' - (Lam. 3:25).

* * * * * * * * * *

CHAPTER 15
JOSEPH'S RELEASE
Gen. 41.

I have told you of the great king of Egypt. He was the king
of the country where Joseph was. His name was Pharaoh. He
had lots of servants, as I told you. He sat upon a throne, wore
beautiful clothes, a chain of gold round his neck, a ring upon
his hand and a crown of gold upon his head. He lived in a fine
house and rode out in a chariot drawn by many horses. As he
passed by people bowed down to the ground. One night, this
great king had two very strange dreams. I will tell you what
they were.

He thought he was standing by a river and that seven fat

cows came out of the river and began to eat the grass that
grew near by. This was a pleasant sight but soon after he saw
seven very thin cows (more ugly than any cows he had ever
seen) come out of the river. They ate up the seven fat cows
yet, after they had eaten them, they looked as thin as they did
before. Then the king awoke.

But soon he fell asleep and dreamt that he saw a stalk of
corn with seven fat ears growing on it. While he was looking
he saw another stalk with seven very bad ears of corn on it and
these bad ears ate up the seven good ears.

These were Pharaoh's two dreams. He thought they were
very strange and longed to know the meaning of them. In the
morning he told the servants to find some people who said
they could tell the meaning of dreams. Lots of men came who
pretended to be wise but they could not tell the king the meaning
of his dreams. The king was very unhappy but what could he
do?

At last the butler thought of Joseph. He had not thought of
him for a long time and now he felt sorry. He said to the king,
"I do remember my faults this day. You know, O king, that
you were once angry with me and with your baker and you
shut us up in prison, in the house of the captain of the guard.
While we were in prison, the baker and I each had a dream
and a young man, a servant, told us the meaning of our dreams.
He said that the baker would be hanged and that I should be
let out of prison and so it was; the baker was hanged and you
sent for me to be your butler again, just as the young man had
said." Then Pharaoh told his servants to fetch this young man
out of prison.

So the servants came to the prison and said to the keeper,
"We have come to fetch Joseph; the king wants to speak to
him."

Joseph must have been glad to hear this. He saw that God

had heard his prayer. Joseph was dressed in very poor clothes, not fit for a king to see. So the servants gave him neat clothes and brought him to the king.

It was a long, long time since Joseph had felt the air blow upon his face and since he had seen the green fields. I think he must have looked pale and sick.

He came into the king's fine house and stood before him. The king said, "I hear that you can tell the meaning of dreams."

"It is not mI," said Joseph, "that can tell the meaning but my God can and I know that he will tell me the meaning of your dreams." Then Pharaoh told Joseph his two dreams - the dream about the seven cows and the dream about the seven ears.

When he had finished speaking Joseph answered, "Both your dreams have the same meaning. This is what is going to happen. The next seven years a great deal of corn will grow in the fields but afterwards hardly any corn will grow in the fields for seven years. The seven fat cows meant the seven years when much corn would grow and the seven thin cows meant the seven years when very little corn would grow. God sent you these dreams that you might know what is going to happen."

Now what could the king do? First, there would be a great deal of corn, then scarcely any. Could you advise the king what to do? Joseph gave him some advice. He said, "Save up some of the corn when there is plenty so that you may have some when there is none growing in the fields. You should look for a very wise man who will save up the corn and put it in large barns; or the people will die when no corn grows in the fields."

Pharaoh was very pleased with Joseph for telling him the meaning of his dreams. He believed what Joseph had said. So then Pharaoh said to his servants, "Where can I find so wise a man as Joseph? He shall save up the corn."

Then Pharaoh said to Joseph, "You are so very wise that you shall help me to manage all the people in the land. Every one shall obey you as they do me and you will be the greatest person next to me."

Then Pharaoh took the ring off his hand and put it on Joseph's hand and he gave him beautiful clothes like his own and a gold chain to wear round his neck. He gave him a fine chariot to ride in and commanded people to bow down when they saw him.

So Joseph was made a great lord but he would not be lazy. For seven years he went about all of the country in his chariot buying corn and building large barns everywhere to store the corn in. He did not spend his time partying - eating and drinking - but always doing good to people.

He was very glad he was let out of prison and he thanked God very much. He was not happy because he wore fine clothes but just glad to be able to do good to people by saving up corn. He married and had two little boys, yet still he thought of his dear old father and hoped that he would see him again one day. He also thought of little Benjamin and hoped his brothers had not killed him, or put him in a pit and he hoped that his brothers were sorry for their wickedness. He did not feel angry with his brothers. Joseph knew that it was God who had let them sell him as a slave and that God had let them do it, so that he might save up corn in Egypt.

It is God that makes all things happen[1] and God has wise reasons for all that he does. If he lets us become ill it is for some good reason. One day we shall know why God lets us become ill, or lets wicked people hurt us, or takes away our things.

You know why God let wicked people kill the Lord Jesus. It was that he might die instead of us and save us from hell.

Questions for Chapter 15

What two dreams did Pharaoh, king of Egypt, have one night?
Who advised him to send for Joseph?
Why was Joseph able to tell him the meaning of the dreams?
What was the meaning of the dreams?
What did Joseph advise the king to do, to prevent the people
from being starved when no corn should grow?
Why did Pharaoh make Joseph the ruler over the people?

Scripture Verse

Who is it that makes all things happen?
'The Lord maketh poor and maketh rich. He bringeth low and
lifteth up.' - (1 Sam. 2:7).

Notes for Chapter 15

[1.] Amos 3:6.

* * * * * * * * * *

CHAPTER 16
JOSEPH THE LORD OF EGYPT
Gen. 42.

You have heard how Joseph was made almost as great as
the king. A great deal of corn grew in the fields the next year
and the year after and for seven years after the king's dream.
But then hardly any corn grew. The poor people came to king
Pharaoh and said, "We have nothing to eat and we shall die."
Then Pharaoh said, "Go to Joseph. He can help you." So the
people went to Joseph and he opened his large barns full of
corn and sold the corn to the people. They brought money
and large bags or sacks. Joseph took the money and filled the

sacks with corn. Lots of people came to buy corn. Some came from a long way off but Joseph had enough corn for all.

Among the people who came there were ten men who had come from a far country. Each of them had a donkey and on the donkey a sack and in their hands they had brought money. Who do you think they were? They were Joseph's brothers. When Joseph saw them he remembered them, although he had not seen them for twenty years. He knew those cruel brothers who had sold him for twenty pieces of silver. If he wanted to he could have punished them. He could have told his servants to kill them. Do you think Joseph punished his brothers, or do you think he was kind to them? Now you shall hear how he behaved to them.

The brothers thought Joseph was a great lord. They did not know recognise him because he wore fine clothes and had grown to be a man with another name; a name the king had given him.

So when the ten brothers saw him they bowed down to the ground before him. Then Joseph remembered his dream about the sheaves bowing down to his sheaf and he saw that God had made it come true.

Joseph felt ready to forgive his brothers but he wanted first to see whether they were sorry for their wickedness and whether they loved their father and little Benjamin. So Joseph did not tell them who he was. He even pretended to be unkind. He spoke to them in a rough voice and said, "Where do you come from?"

"From the land of Canaan," they said, "to buy food."

But Joseph said he did not believe they spoke the truth. "You come," he said, "to see what a bad land this is, with no corn growing in it and you mean to bring some king with soldiers to fight us."

"No," said Joseph's brothers, "we do not. We are ten poor brothers and we have come to buy food."

But Joseph said he would not believe what they said.

Joseph's brothers answered, "We are all brothers and once there were twelve of us but one is dead and the youngest is with our father, who is an old man." They tried to make Joseph believe what they said but he would not; that is, he pretended not to believe them.

Joseph said, "I must see your youngest brother. I will send one of you to fetch him and I will keep the rest in prison till he comes back with the youngest brother."

The brothers were very frightened when they heard this for they knew their father would not choose to part with Benjamin in case he would be killed. So not one of the brothers said he would go and fetch Benjamin.

Joseph put them all in prison and kept them locked up together for three days. While they were there they had time to think of their wickedness to Joseph.

When people are locked away they have time to think and to pray. I hope when you are in your room as punishment that you pray to God to make you good. The brothers were very frightened; they did not know what Joseph was going to do with them.

Joseph came to them in the prison and said, "This is what you must do and then you shall live because I fear God."

How surprised the brothers must have been when they heard Joseph say that he feared God! For the other people in Egypt worshipped idols.

Joseph said, "I will only keep one of you shut up in the prison and all the rest of you may go back and take the corn home with you. However, when you come again you must bring your youngest brother with you or I will think that you haven't told the truth. But, if you do bring him, I will believe you."

The brothers were glad to think that they might go back, yet it made them sad to hear that one of them would be kept in prison. They remembered their wickedness to Joseph and they said one to another, "It was very wicked of us to treat Joseph as we did. How he begged us to spare him and we would not and now God is punishing us for it."

Joseph heard what they said and it made the tears run down his cheeks so that he had to go out of the room to cry. He did not like to see them unhappy but you know he wanted to find out whether they were kind to Benjamin and whether they loved their old father and whether they were sorry for all they had done.

When Joseph came back he took one of the brothers, called Simeon and said that he would keep him in prison till the others brought their youngest brother with them. So Joseph had Simeon tied with ropes, or chains, while the other brothers stood round.

Then they must have remembered how once poor Joseph had been bound and sold for a slave.

Simeon was left alone in the prison and did not know whether his brothers would ever come back and whether he would ever be let out.

Before the brothers set off to go home Joseph said to his servants, "When you fill those men's sacks with corn, put back into their sacks the money that they paid me for it and give also them something to eat on the way." Joseph wanted his poor brothers to have some food on the way home. The servant did as Joseph told him but Joseph's brothers did not know what the servant had done.

How glad these brothers were to get out of Egypt and to come back to their father and little children, who had hardly anything left to eat!

When they had come home they told their father all that had happened. "There was a great lord," they said, "who sold corn to the people and he spoke harshly to us. He said that we were not come to buy corn but that we only wanted to see the land that we might bring men to fight the poor hungry people that lived there. He called us spies. We told him that we were not spies but twelve brothers, although one was dead and one was with our father in the land of Canaan. But that lord would not believe us and told us we must bring our youngest brother with us. He took Simeon and shut him up in prison and said that he wouldn't let him out untill we came back with Benjamin."

Poor old Jacob was very sad when he heard all this. Then the brothers began to open their sacks of corn and they were astonished to find their money at the top of their sacks. However, they were not pleased because they thought that someone had put the money there to get them into trouble and that when they went back to Egypt they would be punished for stealing. So they were very frightened.

They had not stolen this money but they were thieves because they once had stolen Joseph and sold him for twenty pieces of silver. God knew that they were thieves.

They were more afraid than ever of going back to Egypt and of seeing the great lord. however, they had used all the food they had bought and needed more and they knew that poor Simeon would remain in prison untill they went back to Egypt.

How could they persuade Jacob to let Benjamin go? For Jacob said, "No, I cannot trust Benjamin with you, in case some harm should come to him. You have taken away two of my children, Joseph and Simeon, and you would not bring Benjamin back if I were to let him go. If anything bad were to happen to him, you would bring down my grey hairs with sorrow to the grave." Jacob felt that it would break his heart to lose Benjamin. He loved him so very much.

So the brothers had to stay in Canaan for they knew it would be of no use to go to Egypt unless Benjamin went with them. What trouble they were now in! God was punishing them for their wickedness.

Questions for Chapter 16

When no corn grew in the fields, to whom did people go for corn?

Did Joseph recognised his brothers again when he saw them?

Did they recognise him?

Why did they not recognise him again?

How did Joseph's dream about the sheaves come true?

Why did Joseph speak unkindly to his brothers?

What did he say they had come for?

Where did he keep them for three days?

Whom did Joseph want them to bring the next time they came?

Which of the brothers did Joseph keep in prison while the others went to get Benjamin?

What did Joseph desire his servants to put into his brothers' sacks with the corn?

Why were the brothers frightened when they found the money in their sacks?

Why would Jacob not let Benjamin go with his brothers to Egypt?

Scripture Verse

How God saves the righteous and punishes the wicked.
'The righteous is delivered out of trouble and the wicked cometh in his stead.' - (Prov. 11:8).

CHAPTER 17
JOSEPH, OR THE FEAST.
Gen. 43.

As the brothers could not persuade Jacob to let Benjamin go with them. So they felt they had to stay in Canaan. Soon they had eaten up all their corn and none grew in their fields. What could they do for food?

Jacob saw how hungry they were and said, "Go and buy us food again."

Then they said, "We cannot go without Benjamin because the man who sold the corn said we were not to see him unless we brought our youngest brother. If you will let Benjamin come with us, then we will go."

Jacob was very unhappy when he heard this and he said, "Why did you tell the man you had a brother? Telling him this was an inconsiderate thing to do."

Then the brothers answered, "The man asked us so many questions. He said to us, "Is your father alive? Have you another brother? We didn't think that he would say, "Bring your youngest brother?"

Still Jacob did not like to let Benjamin go.

One of the brothers (called Judah) said, "I will take care of Benjamin, if you will let him go. I promise to bring him back to you and if I do not, I will take all the blame. We and our little children shall die if you do not let him come."

Jacob saw it was no use to refuse any more because they would all die, including Benjamin. So he gave Benjamin into the care of Judah.

But Jacob was afraid of the man being unkind to them and

about his saying they had stolen the money. So he said to them, "Take the man a present."

What could they take? They had gardens with fruit and flowers growing in them.

"Pick some nuts and almonds off your trees," said Jacob "and take some of that sweet stuff called balm and myrrh, take some spices, a little honey. Take them with you as a present to the man." Jacob knew that the man was very rich and that he did not want anything but he sent a present to show that he wanted to please him.

"Also," said Jacob, "take back the money that you found in your sacks - take more money to buy more corn and take Benjamin and go to the man."

Jacob's heart was full of pain when he said this.

Then he began to pray to God, "May God give you mercy before the man and send home Simeon and Benjamin!"

This was Jacob's prayer.

"Now," he said, "if I must lose my children, I must lose them!"

When Jacob wished his dear Benjamin good-bye he must have thought of how he once had parted with his Joseph, the day he sent him to look for his brothers - the day when he put on his pretty coat and never returned.

Now Jacob was afraid that he would never see Benjamin again.

The brothers took the present with them and they each took some money, their donkeys, their empty sacks and Judah took care of Benjamin.

So they left their old father, their wives, their little children and they set out on their journey.

They all felt very sad that day. The brothers were frightened. They were afraid they would be imprisoned as thieves when they got to Egypt.

Eventually, they arrived in Egypt. They went to the place where Joseph was selling the corn. Joseph saw them. He looked to see whether Benjamin was with them. How pleased he was to see him!

Benjamin was a baby when Joseph had seen him last yet Joseph knew that it was Benjamin.

As soon as he saw his brothers he called his chief servant who managed his house and said to him, "Take those ten men to my house and get a great dinner ready; they must dine with me to-day."

The brothers did not hear what Joseph said to the servant.

The servant went to them and told them to come with him. So he brought them to Joseph's house - a beautiful, large house. Yet the brothers were not pleased but very frightened.

"Oh no!" they said to each other, "we are going to be put in prison and we will be kept in prison to work hard."

They thought of their poor father and of what he would do.

When they got to the door of the house, they came up to the servant and said, "O sir, we came here once before to buy a little food and we paid money for it but when we got home we opened our sacks and found the money back in our sacks. See, we have brought it back and have brought more money to buy more corn. We don't know who put the money in our sacks."

It was quite right of the brothers to bring the money back but once they had stolen money. Now they were speaking the truth but once they had told lies.

The servant answered them very kindly and said, "Don't be afraid, God is your father. God gave you that money and put it into your sacks."

You see the servant knew about God. Who could have taught him about God? The people in Egypt worshipped idols. It must have been Joseph who had taught his servant.

How happy the brothers were now! They soon found that they were not going to be put into a prison but that they were to dine in a beautiful house. What could make the man grow so kind? They did not know the reason.

While they were waiting, the servant went and brought poor Simeon out of prison. He had been shut up a long time. I hope when he was in prison that he thought about the time he put Joseph in the pit.

The servant told them that dinner would not be ready till twelve o'clock. While they were waiting he brought them water to wash their feet and gave some food to their poor, tired and hungry donkeys.

The brothers said, "Let us get our present ready while we are waiting for the Lord to come in."

So they went out and got the balm and spices, the honey, nuts and almonds ready.

Joseph came in from selling the corn and the brothers came into the house with the present in their hands and bowed down upon the ground. The eleven brothers bowed down as the eleven sheaves of corn had done in Joseph's dream.

This time Joseph spoke very kindly to them. He asked them how they were but most of all he wanted to know how his dear father was.

"Is your father well?" he asked. "You said you had an old father. Is he still alive?"

They said, "Yes, our father is well and he is alive." As they spoke they bowed down their heads to the ground.

Then Joseph looked for Benjamin. When he saw him he longed to throw his arms round his neck and kiss him but he would not do it then. He only said, "Is this your younger brother that you told me about?"

And then he said this little prayer, "God be gracious to you my son."

When Joseph had said this he felt the tears coming into his eyes and he could not help crying. So he went quickly out of the room and shut himself in his own room. There he cried by himself. He was a very tender-hearted man and he loved this young brother very much.

One reason why he loved him was because Benjamin was the son of his own mother, Rachel, while the others had another mother, Leah. Jacob, you know, had two wives.

Now the dinner was ready so Joseph had to leave his room but first he washed his face so that no one might see that he had been crying. Then he tried to look cheerful and he said to his servants, "Put the dinner on the table."

In the room where they were going to eat there were three tables. One was for Joseph's servants, another was for Joseph himself (for he always dined at a table by himself), the other table was for the eleven brothers.

Joseph told them where to sit. He made the eldest sit first and then the second, just according to their age. He made Benjamin sit last. The brothers were surprised that Joseph knew who was the eldest and who was second. It is hard to tell how old a grown-up man is but Joseph knew them better than they thought he did.

Now they all sat down to dinner. It was a long time since they had eaten such a dinner. They had made a great journey and were tired, hungry and thirsty. Joseph sent them nice things from his table but he sent five times as much to Benjamin as to any of the others. They ate and drank and were happy.

Joseph could see them all and it was a pleasant sight to him. Once they had eaten their dinner while he lay in the pit and they had given him none. Yet he would not treat them like that but would return good for evil.

You remember how kindly Jesus behaved to people who were unkind to him. God is kind to us, though we do many things to offend him. If a child is unkind to you should you be unkind too? If your brother has a cake and will not give you any and if afterwards you have a cake should you give him some or should you not? Oh! You should do as Joseph did and be kind to those who have been unkind to you.

Questions for Chapter 17

Who promised Jacob to take care of Benjamin if Jacob would let him go into Egypt?

What did Jacob advise his sons to take with them?

When the brothers came to Egypt where did Joseph's servant bring them?

Why were the brothers so frightened?

Who eventually told them who had put the money in their sacks?

When Joseph came into the house how did the brothers show their respect for him?

What did Joseph say when he saw Benjamin?

Why did Joseph cry?

Who sat at each of the three tables?

To which of the brothers was Joseph the most kind?

Were the brothers envious of Benjamin?

Whom was Joseph like when he was kind to his unkind brother?

Scripture Verse

About forgiving others.

'...if any man have a quarrel against any; even as Christ forgave you, so also do ye.' - (Col. 3:13).

CHAPTER 18
JOSEPH THE FORGIVING BROTHER
Gen. 44; 45:1-15.

The brothers spent a happy day with Joseph. They did not go home that day but waited to set out on the next.

You know that they had come to buy corn and they had brought empty sacks with them. Joseph called his servant and said to him secretly, "Fill the sacks of those eleven men with corn and put their money that they have given me for the corn back into their sacks. And put my silver cup into the sack of the youngest."

The servant filled the sacks with corn and put the money into them. And then he put the silver cup into Benjamin's sack and gave the sacks to the brothers. They did not know that the servant had put money or a cup into them.

The next morning, as soon as it was light, the brothers rose up, took their donkeys and their sacks and set off to return home to their father. How glad they were to get away safely - not one left behind!

What a pleasant story they thought they would have to tell their father! How surprised he would be to hear of the great lord's kindness - and how glad he would be to see Benjamin again!

But soon all their joy turned into grief.

They had gone but a little way when someone called them. It was Joseph's servant. He had come running after them.

"What has made you behave so ill to my lord after all his kindness to you?" he said, "Why have you stolen the silver cup out of which he drinks?"

The brothers were much surprised to hear that the cup was stolen.

"Why do you think," they said, "that we have taken it? We would not do such a wicked thing. Did we not bring back the money when we thought it had been put in our sacks by mistake? Why would we steal a silver cup out of your lord's house? None of us have taken it. If one of us has taken it let him die and let all the rest of be slaves to your lord."

They said this because they were quite sure that none of them had taken it.

"No," said the servant, "it will not be so; the one who has taken the cup will not be killed. He will only be a slave to my lord and the others will not be slaves; they will all go home."

Then the servant told them to open their sacks so the eldest brother took down his sack. The servant looked in amongst the corn but could find no cup. Then the second opened his sack but there was no cup in it. The third showed his and each brother showed his in turn. Finally, Benjamin showed his. How surprised they were when they found the silver cup in it!

You know that Benjamin had not stolen it. You know that the servant had put it in the sack when he filled it with corn.

The servant said to Benjamin, "You must come back with me to my lord." He was going to take him for a slave and never let him return home but he said that his brothers might go home.

And would they go and leave Benjamin behind?

"No," they said, "we will go back with Benjamin."

You see that they loved Benjamin and that they would not leave him alone in his distress.

They put their sacks again on their donkeys and followed the servant to Joseph's house. Their hearts must have been bursting with grief as they went.

Joseph was in his house waiting for them. He was very

glad to see them all come back with Benjamin and to see their grief lest Benjamin should be kept to be a slave. Now Joseph saw that they loved their father very much.

When they saw Joseph they fell with their faces on the ground.

Joseph spoke to them as if he was angry and said, "What is this wicked thing that you have done?"

Do you remember that Judah had promised to take care of Benjamin? So Judah began to beg Joseph to forgive Benjamin.

Judah knew that it would be of no use to say that Benjamin had not taken the cup so he only begged Joseph to take pity on them.

"God is punishing us for our sins," said Judah, "and we can say nothing. We must all be your slaves."

"No," said Joseph, "not all; only he who stole the cup, he will be my slave. Let the others go back to their father."

Joseph wanted to see whether the brothers would go back and leave poor Benjamin to be a slave. Judah then came nearer to Joseph and began to beg for Benjamin.

"Let me speak a word to my lord," he said, "and do not be angry with me for I am as afraid of you as I am of the king. When we first came to buy corn you asked us if we had a father and a brother. We told you we had an old father and a little brother that he loved very much indeed. Then you said that we must bring our brother to show you. Then we said we could not because our father would not part with him but you said we must bring him. So when we went back to our father we told him what you had said but he would not let Benjamin go. "No," he said, "I had a dear child that I think was eaten up by a lion or a bear. If I let Benjamin go perhaps some harm will happen to him and then I shall die of grief and these grey hairs will go down with sorrow to the grave."

"Then I promised my father that I would take care of Benjamin. I cannot go home without him. If I were to go back without Benjamin we would see our father die. Let me be your slave instead of Benjamin and let him go home to his father because I could not bear to see my father die of grief."

Was it not kind of Judah to say this?

Now Joseph saw that Judah did indeed love Benjamin and his old father. Now Joseph would tell his brothers who he was and would tell them that he had forgiven them.

Joseph felt ready to burst into tears yet he did not go out of the room to weep he had done before but he said to all his servants, "Go out of the room" and Joseph was left alone with his brothers. He cried so loud that all the servants heard him although they were not in the room.

Finally, he said, "I am Joseph. Is my father still alive?"

Were the brothers pleased? No, they were frightened; they could not speak and they dared not come near him. Joseph did not wish to frighten them. He longed to put his arms round them and kiss them. He saw that they were unhappy at the thoughts of their wickedness in having sold him so he tried to comfort them.

"Do not grieve because you sold me," said Joseph. "God let you do it that I might save corn to feed your children. I wish you all to come and live with me here. You must bring my old father with you and your children and I will feed you all. Look at me and you will see that I am indeed your own brother Joseph. It is my mouth that speaks to you. Tell my father what fine things I have in Egypt and bring him here to live with me."

This was the loving way in which Joseph spoke. Then he threw his arms round Benjamin's neck and wept as he kissed him and Benjamin wept too upon Joseph's neck. Afterwards Joseph kissed all his brothers and wept as he kissed each and then his brothers no longer felt afraid of him but began to talk to him. They saw Joseph had completely forgiven them and that he had loved them. They could not have expected such kindness and it made them the more sorry for their own wickedness. You see that Joseph did not make his brothers happy till he found that they were really sorry and had turne from their wickedness.

Jesus Christ forgives us all our sins when we are really sorry! You remember how he forgave that poor woman who washed his feet with her tears and wiped them with the hairs of her head. She was sorry for all her sins and Christ told her he had forgiven her. It is the Holy Spirit who makes people sorry for their sins.[1]

Questions for Chapter 18

What did Joseph's servants ask the brothers if they had stolen?
What did the servant say should be done to the thief?
In whose sack was it found?
Who had put it in Benjamin's sack?
Did the servant allow the brothers to go home to their father?
Why did the brothers return to Joseph with Benjamin?
What did Judah ask Joseph to do instead of keeping Benjamin?
Why did Joseph *then* tell his brothers who he was?
Why were they frightened when they heard he was Joseph?
How did Joseph behave to them?

Scripture Verse

About the kindness of the Lord.
'For thou, Lord, art good and ready to forgive and plenteous in mercy unto all them that call upon thee.' - (Ps. 86:5).

Notes for Chapter 18

[1] Acts 3:19.

CHAPTER 19
JOSEPH THE LONG-LOST SON

Gen. 45:16 to end; 46; 47:1-12; 50.

Before Joseph told his brothers who he was he had sent his servants out of the room but he had sobbed so loud that the servants had heard and soon they knew the reason why Joseph had sent them out. The servants were glad to hear that Joseph had found his brothers. Joseph had not told the people of Egypt of his brothers' wickedness.

Pharaoh, the king, heard of the brothers being found and he too was glad because he loved Joseph.

He called Joseph and said to him, "Your brothers must come and live near you and you must send for your old father and for all the little children. They shall have the best of all the land to eat. We must send wagons to bring the little children, their mothers and your old father but they need not bring their things for we will give them the best of everything of all Egypt.

You see how kind the king was.

Joseph got wagons, with some animals to draw them and he gave his brothers some food to eat as they travelled home. He also made them some beautiful presents because Joseph was very rich. He gave them each two suits of clothes but to Benjamin he gave five suits of clothes, besides a great deal of money. He sent a present to his father; ten donkeys that carried all kinds of good things, then more donkeys that carried a great deal of bread and other food for his father to eat by the way.

When all things were ready Joseph told his brothers to go to Canaan and to come back quickly. He gave them one piece of advice before they went. "Take care," he said, "that you do not quarrel by the way."

They must have had a pleasant journey.

Old Jacob had been longing to see them and very worried Benjamin would not come back safely. At last they came and he saw that not one was missing.

They told him quickly the joyful news. "Joseph is alive and he is the great lord that sells corn in the land of Egypt."

Perhaps you think Jacob was delighted but no - he would not believe them.

"No," he said, "my son has long been dead."

"But we have seen him," they said.

"It cannot be true," said Jacob.

Then the brothers told him what Joseph had said. "He wants us all to come and live with him and he sends for you."

Still Jacob would not believe them.

"Just come and see the waggons he has sent and then you will believe us," they said.

So they took old Jacob to see the waggons and when he saw them he did believe and then he was glad.

"It is enough," said old Jacob. "Joseph my son is yet alive; I will go and see him before I die."

The brothers told their wives and their children that they must leave Canaan and take a long journey. They got into the waggons and set out. Jacob was lame[1] and old and he rode in a waggon but the brothers were strong enough to walk. They took their sheep,cows, goats, camels and donkeys with them and all their things. They had to travel a very long way. No doubt the little children were very pleased because children are like making journeys.

At last they came into the land of Egypt.

Long before they came to Joseph's house they saw a fine chariot coming towards them. It was Joseph's. It stopped and Joseph got out of it.

When Joseph saw his father he ran to meet his father, threw his arms round his neck and then he wept for a long time.

The last time Joseph had kissed his father was when he was a boy, dressed in his pretty coat and was going to look for his brothers to see how they were. How many sad days Jacob had spent thinking of him! And now, at last, he had found him again.

The brothers did not feel envious now when they saw Jacob and Joseph folded in each other's arms.

"Now," said old Jacob, "let me die since I have seen your face, Joseph, once more."

Then Joseph said to his fathers and brothers, "I will go and tell Pharaoh that you have arrived."

So Joseph went to Pharaoh the king and said, "My father and brothers, their flocks and all that they have, have arrived."

And then he brought five of his brothers and showed them to Pharaoh. And Pharaoh said to them, "What is your employment?"

"We are shepherds but there is a hard famine in Canaan and no pasture for our sheep. Can we settle in Goshen?"

Pharaoh said that he would give them this land with pasture and that they might live there all together with their children and their flocks.

Joseph wanted them to live all together because the people in Egypt worshipped idols.

Joseph wanted the king to see his dear old father so he brought him to the king. The king treated him with great respect, because Jacob was a very old man. Even kings should pay respect to old men.

Should not children pay great respect to an old man! When they see an old man they should be ready to help him and to do what he tells them.

Jacob was introduced to Pharaoh and blessed him.

Pharaoh then said to Jacob, "How old are you?"

Jacob said, "I am one hundred and thirty years old but I am not as old as my fathers were and my life has been full of troubles."

Then Jacob blessed Pharaoh again and went away to the place Pharaoh had given him to live in. There he lived with all his children round him. Joseph did not live with him but he often came to see him.

Jacob eventually, fell sick and knew that he would soon die. He sent for all his sons that he might bless them before he died. Jacob had been lame a long time and now he was almost blind, very weak and sick.

When his sons came he sat upon the bed and called them one by one that he might give a blessing to each. After he had blessed them he said, "I am soon going to die; bury me in the cave in Canaan where Abraham, my grandfather, is buried and Isaac, my father.

He said a great deal more and then finally, he died.

His spirit went to God and he is still with him in heaven. His body will rise from the cave at the last day.

Joseph fell upon his father's face when he was dead and wept upon him and kissed him. Those grey hairs had not gone down in sorrow to the grave for God had comforted Jacob before he died.

Joseph took his father's body to Canaan to put it in the cave where Abraham and Isaac were. All the brothers went with Joseph and many servants and chariots and horses. Afterwards they came back to Egypt.

A very sad thought came into the minds of the brothers. They said to each other, "Perhaps Joseph has only been so kind to us to please his father. Perhaps he has not really forgiven us and now perhaps he will punish us." So they sent a servant to Joseph and told the servant to say to Joseph, "Your father, before he died, told us to beg you to forgive us our great wickedness. So pray forgive us."

When Joseph heard this message he began to weep. Why did he weep? Because he was sorry that his brothers should think he could be so unkind to them. Soon his brothers came and fell down before him and seemed much afraid. Joseph said, "Fear not; it was wrong of you to sell me yet God made it turn out for good because when I was in Egypt I saved the corn and so you were kept from dying from hunger. I will still feed you and your little children." He spoke very kindly to them and comforted them.

Joseph lived to be a very old man and eventually, he died.

This is the history of Joseph. He is now in heaven with his dear Lord. Joseph forgave his brothers and Christ has forgiven him because Joseph committed sins although they are not written down in the Bible.

You have heard the history of Abraham, Isaac and Jacob. God loved all three of them. Abraham was the grandfather, Isaac the father and Jacob the son.

God had promised the land of Canaan to the children of Abraham, Isaac and Jacob; that is, to their great-great-grand-children. God would not forget that promise. But he had made them a better promise. He had promised them that one day the Christ would be born into the world and would save them from their sins.[2] Abraham, Isaac and Jacob[3] often looked forward with faith to God's promise even though they did not know it would be fulfilled in Jesus.[4]

Fianlly, Christ did come and now Christ is in heaven. So is Abraham, Isaac and Jacob, as well as Abel, Noah and Joseph and all good people who wait to be made perfect with those whose sins Christ has forgiven.[5] Oh, may you be with them one day!

Questions for Chapter 19

Whom did Pharaoh invite to live in Egypt?

Why was Jacob not pleased when he first heard that Joseph was alive?

What eventually made Jacob believe that Joseph was alive?

How did the little children make such a long journey into Egypt?

Who met Jacob on his coming into Egypt?

To whom did Joseph show his old father?

How did Pharaoh treat Jacob?

Where did Jacob and his sons live?

Where did Jacob desire his sons to bury him?

What were the brothers afraid of after Jacob was dead?

Was Joseph as kind after Jacob's death as he had been before?

What was the name of Joseph's father?

And of Jacob's father?

And of Isaac's father?

What was the name of Abraham's wife?

Of Isaac's wife? Of Jacob's wives?

How many sons had Jacob?

What promises had God made to Abraham, Isaac and Jacob?

Scripture Verse

How the young should behave to the old.

'Thou shalt rise up before the hoary head and honour the face of the old man and fear thy God...' - (Lev. 19:32).

Notes for Chapter 19

[1] Gen. 32:31.   [2] Gal. 3:8.   [3] Gen.49:18.
[4] Heb. 11:13; Rom. 15:8.   [5] Heb. 11:40.

SECTION 2

EXODUS

Introduction

Genesis finished with Joseph, his brothers and their families settling in Egypt. In Exodus, we learn that their descendants have grown into a nation; making the Egyptians fear that they will take over the country. The Egyptians made the Israelites become slaves, causing them to cry to God for help.

In this second book of the Bible we learn that God calls a man named Moses to lead the Israelites out of slavery and take them on a journey towards the Promised Land. God begins to teach them all about himself, giving them his commandments and Law. These instructions show the Israelites how to live and more importantly teach them, and those around them, what God is like.

Some Suggestions for Study

We might not be slaves like the Israelites were in Egypt but the Apostle Paul tells us we can be like slaves to sin (Romans 6:6). For example, if we struggle with losing our temper we may be slaves to anger. We could be slaves to other things – wanting money and possessions or thinking that we must have the latest fashions or games. Perhaps we can't stop lying and cheating or being unkind. Before each chapter think about how you might be involved in this kind of slavery. Pray that God will free you so that you might be able to move on as a part of His people.

CHAPTER 20
MOSES AND THE BASKET OF BULRUSHES
Exod. 1; 2:1-10.

You have heard how Joseph and his brothers lived happily in Egypt for a long time. Eventually, they grew old and died but they left lots of children and their children had lots of children till there were hundreds and thousands of people. These people were the grandchildren of Jacob and his great-grandchildren and their children.

Did you know that Jacob had two names? His other name was Israel. It was a name that God had given him.

All the sons of Jacob were called the children of Israel, or the children of Jacob, while the grandchildren of Jacob were called by this same name - "The children of Israel." There were some men, women and some children. All of them together were called "The children of Israel."

The grown-up people were called "The children of Israel."

They did not live in Canaan, you remember. They had left Canaan because no corn grew there for a long time. They lived in Egypt and took care of their sheep. While the good king Pharaoh lived they were very happy. Eventually, he died and there was another Pharaoh as king of Egypt. You shall hear what he did and then you shall tell me whether you think he was good.

He knew that the children of Israel had come from far away and he said, "There are so many of them that perhaps they may some day fight against me with swords and kill me and my servants. I will make them slaves and give them hard work."

So he ordered them to make lots of bricks and build very high walls. He sent some of his men to make them work hard.

The children of Israel were used to taking care of sheep and that is a pleasant employment. Shepherds lead their flocks to the green fields, by the side of the quiet waters and they sit under the shade of a tree when the sun is hot. Isn't this pleasant? But now the children of Israel were obliged to dig up the clay, to make bricks and to dry them in the sun. If they did not make lots of bricks the men whom Pharaoh had sent beat them. So now they were very unhappy; they often sighed, groaned and shed tears.

Yet all this hard work did not stop them multiplying so the king thought of another plan. He said, "Let every boy-baby be thrown into the river." He did not order the baby girls to be drowned because they would not be able to fight with swords when they grew up.

There was a very good woman who had a little baby boy. She was one of the children of Israel.

This woman knew that God would take care of her child and she prayed to God to take care of him. She hid her baby so that Pharaoh's men could not find him. I do not know where she put him but God taught her to hide him in a very safe place.

When the baby was three months old she found that she could not hide him any more. What could she do with her baby?

You have heard of the great river of Egypt. Lots of reads and bulrushes grew, like very high grass, close to the river. She took some bulrushes and made them into a large basket. She wanted to make a basket into which the water would not come. So she got some pitch and covered the basket with it. Then she put her little baby inside and took the basket in her arms. No one could tell what was in the basket.

She went to the riverside and laid the basket among the

great rushes, close by the water. She knew that God would not let the child be killed and so she left him, trusting in God.

She had a little girl of ten years old. This little girl was the baby's sister. She stood far away to see what would become of her baby brother. Soon she saw some ladies walking by the riverside. One of these ladies was king Pharaoh's daughter. She was a princess. The other ladies were her maids and they were going with the princess to some place where she could wash (for Egypt is a very hot country and people often bathe in hot countries).

The princess was looking at the rushes when she saw something very strange peeping out amongst them. When she saw it she said to one of her maids, "Go and see what that is." So the maid went and found the basket. She took it up and brought it to the princess. The princess opened the basket and saw a baby. He was fair and lovely.[1]

He began to weep. Poor infant! He was used to lying in his mother's arms but now there was no one to feed him or to comfort him. The princess pitied the child. She had heard how her father had ordered that every baby was to be thrown into the river and she said, "I suppose this is the baby of one of the children of Israel." She did not want the baby to be thrown into the river.

The baby's sister had come nearer and had seen what the princess had done. She saw that the princess pitied him; so she said, "If you want a nurse, I could find you one who would nurse the child for you." The princess said, "Go."

Whom did she call? The baby's mother. When she had come, the princess said to her, "Take this child and nurse him for me and I will give you wages."

How glad the mother was to care for him! She saw that

God had heard her prayers and saved her child from being drowned.

The mother could teach him about God as soon as he could understand. But she was not allowed to keep him always. When he was a big child the princess sent for him to come and live with her and she called him her son. She gave him a name. "I shall call him 'Moses,'" she said. Moses means, "drawn out." She called him this because he was drawn out of the water.

The princess lived in a beautiful house and had lots of servants. Moses had beautiful clothes, nice things to eat and servants to wait upon him. He had no hard work to do yet he was not idle but learned a great deal of things. The princess told wise men to teach him.

He knew the names of the stars, the animals, the birds and plants. He learned about all these things and grew very wise. One thing these wise men could not teach him was about God for they worshipped idols. Moses knew about God because his father and mother knew the true God and when he was little Moses lived with them. Of all the things Moses knew this was the best. He was wiser than all the men in Egypt for he knew the true God.

He was brave as well as wise and all the people in Egypt praised him and paid him respect. Was Moses happy? No. I will tell you why in the next lesson.

Questions for Chapter 20

What was Jacob's other name?

What name was given to all the children, grandchildren and great-grandchildren of Jacob?

When the Pharaoh who loved Joseph was dead, who was the king of Egypt?

Why did that Pharaoh make the children of Israel work so very hard in making bricks?

What did he order to be done to the baby boys of the children of Israel?

What was it that one of the women did with her baby?

When she could no longer hide it, where did she put it?

Who watched to see what would become of the baby?

Who found the baby?

What did the princess call him?

Whom did she hire to be its nurse?

Whose son was Moses called?

Was Moses rich and great?

What promise had God made to Abraham about his children's children?

Scripture Verse

What the righteous man does in his trouble.
'As for me, I will call upon God and the Lord shall save me.' - (Ps. 55:16).

Notes for Chapter 20

[1.] Acts 7:20.

* * * * * * * * *

CHAPTER 21
MOSES AND THE DECISION
Exod. 2:11-15.

I have told you how very hard the poor children of Israel worked in making bricks. When Moses had grown to be a man he thought, "I live in a beautiful house and I am as important as a prince. I have no work to do but my poor cousins, the children of Israel, are working like slaves. Cruel men are beating them. Can I not help them?" This thought made him sad.

Do you remember the promise God made to Abraham about his great-great-grandchildren? These children of Israel were the great-great-grandchildren of Abraham.

Abraham's child was called Isaac, Abraham's grandchild was Jacob and Abraham's great-grandchildren were Joseph and his brothers. Now Joseph's children were Abraham's great-great-grandchildren and their children were his great-great-great-grandchildren. The children of Israel called Abraham their great-great-great-grandfather but they had never seen him because he died before they were born.

You, my little child, had a great-great-grandfather. I do not know what his name was but I know he has been dead a long time. If he was alive he would call you his great-great-grandchild.

I am now going to tell you about these great-great-grandchildren of Abraham, Isaac and Jacob and about their children and their children. I shall always call them "The children of Israel".

What promise had God made to Abraham about them? He had said that they would live in the land of Canaan - that land, full of hills and rivers, grass and flowers, sheep and cows, milk and honey. God had said to Abraham, "I will give this land to your children." Not to Isaac but to his great-great-great-great-grandchildren, to their children and to their children's children.

Moses had heard of this promise. Perhaps his mother had told him of it. He had heard how he had been saved from being drowned when he was a little baby and he believed that God would let him bring the children of Israel into Canaan. He wanted to save them from being slaves among the wicked people of Egypt and to make them happy in that pleasant land of Canaan. It was kind of Moses to wish to help the poor children of Israel.

Moses left the king's beautiful house and all his beautiful things and he went to the place where the poor children of Israel were working. How sad was the sight he saw! There they were, labouring in the heat of the sun. They worked from morning till night. They dug up the clay to make bricks. That was hard work. Then they made the bricks, putting them in heaps to dry them in the sun. They then carried them to build the great walls for Pharaoh.

They were forced to make many bricks and the cruel men that Pharaoh had sent beat them when they were tired. They groaned and cried but still they were made to do their tasks because the men set them a task. It was not such a little task as you have to do but a big task. The men said, "You must make so many bricks." I do not know how many they told them to make but it was a lot. If they did not do their task the men would beat them. Moses was very sorry to see how the poor children of Israel were treated.

One day he saw one of the task-masters (the cruel men were called task-masters) beating one of the children of Israel. Moses could not bear to see the poor slave treated so cruelly. Moses looked to see whether there were any more task-masters near. He saw no more. So he killed the task-master, put him in a hole in the ground and covered it over with the earth.

One of the Israelites saw him and soon king Pharaoh heard of it. Pharaoh was very angry and tried to find Moses so that he might have him killed. So Moses was obliged to flee to a country far away where the king could not find him. I will tell you another time what happened to Moses in that country. God loved Moses and he took care of him wherever he went.

Moses could always have lived in a beautiful house, ridden in a chariot and had many servants but you see how much he loved the poor children of Israel. Do you not think that he was like the Lord Jesus who left his throne in heaven to save us from going to hell?

Moses wanted to please God more than to be called the son of Pharaoh's daughter.[1] He knew that God loved the children of Israel and he knew that God would one day help him to take them into Canaan.

Questions for Chapter 21

When Moses was grown up where did he go?
Where did Moses wish to lead the children of Israel?
What did Moses find them doing?
Who were the taskmasters?
What did Moses do to one of those cruel men?
Was it right of Moses to kill him?
Did anybody see Moses kill him?
Why did Moses go into a country far away?
What might Moses have been if he had chosen it?
Why did he choose rather to help the children of Israel?
Who once left his throne in heaven to save us from Satan?

Scripture Verse

The choice of the righteous.
'...I had rather be a doorkeeper in the house of my God than to dwell in the tents of wickedness.' - (Ps. 84:10).

Notes for Chapter 21

[1] Heb. 11:24-26.

CHAPTER 22
MOSES AND THE BURNING BUSH
Exod. 2:16 to end; 3; 4.

Moses was grieved to leave the poor children of Israel groaning in Egypt but he was forced to hide himself from Pharaoh.

He took nothing with him on his journey - no servant, no donkey - but God was with him. Though he could not see him Moses knew he was near him and this was his comfort.

Eventually, Moses came to a place where there was much grass and many sheep. Here, also, there was a well and Moses sat down by the side of it because he had taken a long journey.

He had no house, no bed and no friend. He was like Jesus, who had nowhere to lay his head. But you will see that God will take care of him.

Soon there came seven girls to the well. They were sisters and they took care of their father's sheep. They brought their sheep with them to give them water. First they let down some pails, or buckets, into the well and then poured the water into some big troughs that stood near and the sheep drank out of the troughs. While they were doing this some shepherds came to the well and tried to drive them away so that their own sheep might drink water out of the troughs. The poor girls had filled the troughs with water so it would have been very unfair to take the water from their sheep. But the men were stronger than they were and often behaved in this way towards them.

Moses did not like to see weak people ill-treated and he was very strong so he stood up and would not let the shepherds send the girls away. Instead he helped them to draw water for their sheep.

The poor girls thought that Moses was very kind because he was only a stranger and yet he had helped them.

When they came home to their father, he said, "How is it that you have come home so soon to-day?" And they said, "A stranger was by the well; he would not let the shepherds drive us away and he drew water for our sheep."

Then the father answered, "Where is the man? Call him and ask him to come and eat bread with us." So the girls called Moses and asked him to come to their house.

It was God who put it into the man's heart to be kind to Moses.

The old father asked Moses to live with him and his daughters and Moses said he would. Moses took care of the old father's sheep and he married one of the seven girls. Then the old father was called Moses' father-in-law because he was the father of his wife.

Moses had once been a fine prince and had ridden in a chariot but now he led sheep to eat grass among the green hills.

There was one thing that must have made Moses sad. What was that? He knew that the children of Israel were still groaning at their hard work. Could he be happy while they were so miserable? You know that he could not because Moses loved these poor people.

The children of Israel were indeed working hard. King Pharaoh had died but there was another king Pharaoh as wicked as he had been.

Eventually, the children of Israel cried to God to help them and God heard their prayers. He remembered the promise made to Abraham and he decided to save them. Now you will hear what God did to help them.

One day Moses was with the old father's sheep, among the high hills. He was quite alone. He looked up and saw a bush on fire. He went on looking and the bush was still burning but was not more burnt away than at first. This surprised him very much and he said, "I will go and look at the bush and see why it is not burnt up."

He was just going up to it, when he heard some one speak. The voice came out of the bush. Whose voice could it be?

It was the voice of God, who said to him, "Moses, Moses!" He answered, "Here I am."

Then God said, "Do not come near this place for I am here. I have heard the children of Israel crying to me in their trouble and I remember that I promised Abraham that his children would live in Canaan and I am going to send them to Canaan. Moses, you must go to Pharaoh and tell him to let them go."

Was this not a hard thing for Moses to do? But God said, "I will be with you and help you."

Then Moses said, "But perhaps the children of Israel will not choose to come out of Egypt. They will say, 'We will not go with you, Moses. You are not speaking the truth, God has not really spoken to you." "What shall I do then?" Moses said.

Then God said that he would teach him to do wonderful things. God said, "What do you hold in your hand?"

Now Moses had a long stick in his hand, called a rod. He used to help his sheep to get out of holes with his rod and when he climbed high hills he leaned upon his rod. So when God said, "What do you hold in your hand?" Moses answered, "A rod."

"Throw it upon the ground," said the Lord. And Moses did so and it was turned into a serpent. Moses was afraid of the serpent and began to run away from it.

Then God said, "Take hold of it by the tail." So Moses took hold of it and it was turned again into a rod.

God said to Moses, "When you go to Egypt do this wonderful thing before the children of Israel to show them that I have sent you. If they will not believe you, do what I will show you. Put your hand in your chest."

So Moses put in his hand and then he drew it out and it was leprous; that is, it was all covered over with white spots. What a frightful sight this was!

Then God said, "Put your hand in again." He put it in and pulled it out again and then it was as well as it was before.

Then God said to Moses, "If the children of Israel will not believe that I have really spoken to you let them see you do this wonder."

"But," said Moses, "I cannot speak well; I do not know the words to say."

Then God told Moses that Aaron, his brother, should go with him and speak for him. You have not heard of Aaron before. He could speak well, was a good man and loved God.[1]

Moses went back to his father-in-law and told him that he must go back to Egypt. He took his wife and his two little sons with him upon a donkey.

As Moses was going to Egypt he met his brother Aaron. Aaron was glad to see him and kissed him. Moses and Aaron then went together to the land of Egypt.

They found the poor Israelites at their hard work, crying and groaning. Aaron said to them, "God has sent us to tell Pharaoh to let you go to the land of Canaan." Then Aaron did the wonders that God had shown Moses when he spoke to him from the bush. You know what wonders I mean.

Did the people of Israel believe what Aaron did? Did they wish to go to the land of Canaan? Yes, they did and they thanked God for hearing their prayers. I have often told you that God hears people's prayers. I hope that you always pray to him when you are unhappy.

The children of Israel did believe and they said, "We will go," and they bowed their heads and thanked the Lord for his goodness.

But Moses could not take them out of Egypt till Pharaoh had given them leave.

Questions for Chapter 22

When Moses ran away from Egypt where did he eventually rest himself?

What kindness did Moses show to seven girls?

What kindness did their father show to Moses?

What work did Moses do?

What wonderful sight did he see while he was leading his sheep?

Where did God tell Moses to go?

Why did God determine to bring the children of Israel into Canaan?

What two wonderful things did God make Moses able to do?

Why did God make Moses able to do these wonderful things?

Who did God tell Moses should speak for him when he got to Egypt?

When Moses and Aaron were come to Egypt what did they say to the children of Israel?

Did the Israelites believe that God had really spoken to Moses?

Did the children of Israel wish to go to Canaan?

Scripture Verse

Why God sent Moses to bring the children of Israel out of Egypt.

'For he remembered his holy promise and Abraham his servant.' - (Ps. 105:42).

Notes for Chapter 22

1. Ps. 106:16.

* * * * * * * * * *

CHAPTER 23
MOSES AND THE FIRST PLAGUES
Exod. 5; 6; 7; 8; 9:1-12.

The next day Moses and Aaron and some of the children of Israel with them, went in to speak to king Pharaoh. He was a proud and wicked man and he worshipped idols.

It was Aaron who spoke to Pharaoh. He said, "The Lord God commands you to let the children of Israel go."

Do you think Pharaoh did let them go? No. He spoke proudly and said, "Who is the Lord, that I should obey his voice? I know not the Lord, neither will I let Israel go." This was his proud answer.

He was now more unkind than before to the children of Israel and ordered the task-masters to make them work harder so that the children of Israel cried still more bitterly.

As Moses and Aaron came out from king Pharaoh, they saw some Israelites waiting for them. These men said to Moses and Aaron, "You have only done us harm by asking Pharaoh to let us go. He makes us work harder than ever."

It was ungrateful of the children of Israel to speak in this manner to Moses who had tried to help them. Moses was very meek and gentle and he did not answer angrily. Instead he went and prayed to God and asked what he must do now.

God told him to go in to king Pharaoh and to show him the wonder of the serpent. So Moses and Aaron went in. Moses said to Aaron, "Take this rod and throw it on the ground!"

And Aaron threw it down and it became a live snake. Afterwards it turned into a rod again.

Would Pharaoh now say he would let Israel go? No, he would not; his heart was very hard and he cared for nothing.

So God told Moses to do another wonderful thing. I will tell you what it was.

Early in the morning Moses and Aaron went down to the side of the great river and waited there till Pharaoh came because he often came there to bathe. Then they said to him, "Because you would not do as God commanded and let Israel go, now you shall see what God can do."

Then Aaron took the rod and lifted it up over the water. In a moment, the water was turned into blood.

When Pharaoh saw this wonder, did he say that he would let the people go? No; his heart was very hard and he would not obey God. Pharaoh turned back, went into his house and would not obey God.

The people of Egypt had nothing to drink for all the water in the ponds had turned into blood and all the water in jugs and basins and cups had also turned into blood. The fish in the river died and a very bad smell came from the river. The people dug holes in the ground to get water. The water was blood for a whole week.

As Pharaoh would not change his mind God sent him another plague.

Aaron stretched out the rod and frogs came running out of the river and out of the ponds, hundreds and hundreds of frogs. They ran into the streets and into the houses and went into the bedrooms and into the beds. They went into the kitchens and got among the food. They went even into Pharaoh's house and into his bed.

Then Pharaoh called for Moses and Aaron and said to them,

"Pray to God to take away the frogs. I will let the children of Israel go."

Moses went and prayed to God. God made all the frogs die so that the people swept the dead frogs into heaps and these heaps had a very bad smell.

But still Pharaoh said, "I will not let the people go."

So God sent another plague.

Aaron stretched out the rod and turned all the dust into nasty little insects that crawled over the men and over the animals However, Pharaoh would still not change his mind.

Then God sent swarms of flies that came in at the windows and spoiled everything, indoors and out of doors. But no flies came near the children of Israel.

Then Pharaoh said, "I will let the children of Israel go, if God will take away the flies." Then Moses prayed to God and God took all the flies away and did not even leave one. Then Pharaoh said, "I will not let the people go."

So another plague was sent.

The animals fell very sick - the horses and donkeys, the camels, the cows and the sheep - and many of them died. Yet Pharaoh would not let the people go.

Afterwards God made many boils come upon the men, women and children but not upon the children of Israel, only upon Pharaoh's people. They were so sick that they could not stand; yet Pharaoh would not change his mind because his heart grew harder and harder.

I have now told you of six plagues. Try and remember what they were.

1. Water turned into blood.
2. Frogs.
3. Small insects.
4. Flies.

5. Death of the animals.
6. Boils.

I shall soon tell you of some more plagues that God sent to Pharaoh.

God was much stronger than Pharaoh and was able to make him do what he commanded him to do. Wasn't it very wicked of Pharaoh not to listen to God? And was it not very foolish of Pharaoh not to obey so great a God!

God will punish everybody who does not obey his commands.

God has given you many commands. He has told you not to tell lies, to lose your temper or to be unkind. I hope you will try to obey God's commands. For if you think in your heart, as Pharaoh did, "Who is the Lord, that I should obey his voice?" - will not God be very angry with you?

Questions for Chapter 23

When Moses and Aaron asked Pharaoh to let Israel go to Canaan, what did Pharaoh answer?

What was the first thing Moses and Aaron did to show Pharaoh that God had sent them?

Why did God turn the water into blood?

Repeat the six plagues I have told you of?

Scripture Verse

Whom should we fear?

'Thou, even thou, art to be feared and who may stand in thy sight when once thou art angry?' - (Ps. 76:7).

CHAPTER 24
MOSES AND THE LAST PLAGUES
Exod. 9:13; 10; 11; 12.

One morning Moses and Aaron rose up very early and came to Pharaoh and said to him, "Tomorrow God is going to rain great hailstones from the sky - such hailstones as were never seen in Egypt before. They will kill all men and creatures that are outdoors. Therefore you must keep your cows, horses and donkeys in the stables or they will be killed."

Many of the men of Egypt heard Moses and Aaron say this. Some of them believed their words. They kept their animals in their stables and told their servants to keep indoors. But some of the men who heard did not believe and let their animals remain in the fields and their servants with them.

The next day Moses stretched out his rod towards the sky and God sent thunder, hail and fire which ran along the ground. It was a most dreadful storm. Such a storm was never seen before. The noise of the hailstones and of the thunder must have made everyone who heard it tremble. But how glad those must have been who were in their houses! Many creatures and men were killed, grass and corn were burnt up by the fire and the trees were broken. Yet there was no hail where the children of Israel were.

This storm frightened Pharaoh and he sent for Moses and Aaron and said, "I have sinned; only pray the Lord to send no more thunder and hail and I will let the children of Israel go."

Moses said, "I will go out of the city, stretch out my hands to God and he will not send any more thunder and hail but still I know you will not obey God yet."

So Moses went out of the city for he did not fear the storm.

Then he stretched out his hands and God made the hail and thunder stop and he made the rain leave off.

Did Pharaoh let Israel go? No; when he saw that the storm was over he would not. All Pharaoh's servants were wicked too because they did not want him to let the Israelites go.

Then Moses and Aaron went to king Pharaoh again and said, "God will now send locusts into your country."

What are locusts? They are insects about the size of a child's thumb. Thousands of them fly close together in the air, they perch upon the trees and eat up all the leaves and fruit.

Pharaoh and the servants were very angry when they heard that the locusts were coming. They spoke roughly to Moses and Aaron and drove them out of the house.

Moses stretched out the rod and God made the wind blow very hard. The next day the wind blew a great number of locusts into Egypt. The locusts made the sky look black as the wind blew them along but they did not stay in the air. They perched on the trees and ate up the fruit that the hail had left. They covered the grass and ate it up and they even came into the houses.

Pharaoh and his servants thought that they should soon have nothing to eat. Pharaoh sent quickly for Moses and Aaron. "I have sinned," he said, "against the Lord and against you. Only forgive me this once and pray to God to take away the locusts and I will let Israel go."

So Moses prayed to the Lord. God sent another wind and it blew the locusts away. They fell into the sea and there was not one locust left in Egypt.

But Pharaoh still said, "I will not let Israel go."

How sad it must have been to have walked in the fields after the locusts had been there! It was the pleasant spring but it looked like winter. There were no leaves on the trees, there was no tender grass; all was bare as in winter. What misery had Pharaoh's wickedness brought upon the land!

The next time Moses did not tell Pharaoh what God was going to do. Moses stretched out his rod towards heaven and in one moment God made it dark. It was darker than ever it is at night. There was not the least light, except where the children of Israel lived; there it was quite light.

The people of Egypt were very much frightened. They were doing their work, or cating, or walking, when all at once this darkness came on. They stopped, sat down in the place where they were and never moved, night or day. Now they had time to think of all their wickcdness.

It was dark for three days and three nights and then it grew light.

But was Pharaoh sorry for his wickedness? No; his heart was harder than ever. He said to Moses, "Get away! You shall never see my face again. If you come to mc any more you shall die."

Then Moses said, "You shall see my face no more."

God spoke to Moses again and said, "I am going to send another plague. At night I shall come into every house in Egypt and kill the eldest son of every person. But this is what I desire the children of Israel to do. Let each man take a lamb, a lamb without spot, kill it and eat it that night with his family. Let them take the blood of the lamb and put some blood outside the door. When I pass I shall see the blood and I will not kill the eldest son in that house. Let the people in the house stand round the table while they eat the lamb. Let them all be dressed ready for a journey."

So all the children of Israel killed young lambs, roasted them and ate them at night. They stood round their tables with their sticks in their hands. They ate some bread and some bitter herbs with the lamb. They did not forget to put some blood on the posts of the door for then they knew they were safe.

The men of Egypt went to bed that night as usual but in the middle of the night the eldest son in each house died. No one saw God's angel enter in but he did come. No bars or bolts could keep him out but when he saw the blood on the door then he passed over the house.

What a dreadful cry the fathers and mothers made in Egypt when they found their eldest sons were dead! They rushed out of their houses weeping. "Our darling son is dead!" said one. "And so is mine!" said another. "And mine!" "And mine!" There never was such dreadful crying heard in Egypt before.

Even Pharaoh's eldest son was killed as well as the sons of the poor people. Pharaoh rose up at night and called for Moses and Aaron but it was dark so that they did not see his face.

"Go," said Pharaoh, "and take the children of Israel with you; they may take their sheep and cows with them and all that they have."

And all the men of Egypt begged the children of Israel to go away as fast as possible because they were afraid that God would kill them all. Then the Israelites said to the women of Egypt, "Do give us some gold and silver before we go."[1]

And they said, "We will give you what you want; just go!"

The Israelites had done a great deal of work in Egypt and it was right that they should have some money given to them.

So the women of Egypt gave them many beautiful things to take with them.

The Israelites went away in a great hurry. They took their things just as they were. They put bread in their bags, they drove their sheep, cows, camels and donkeys before them and so they set out in the night.

There was a great crowd of people. No little child could have counted them.

So, eventually, they came out of Egypt where they had been slaves so long. God had remembered his promise to Abraham and Abraham's children were on their way to the land of Canaan.

God said to Moses, "They must never forget my kindness in bringing them out of Egypt. They must eat a lamb every year as they have done tonight. Eating the lamb shall be called eating the Feast of the Passover." Why was this supper called the Passover? Because God passed over the doors where the blood was seen.

Of whom does the lamb that each family killed make you think? Of Jesus. That lamb's blood saved the eldest son in the family from being killed and Jesus' blood saves all people who love him from being punished in hell. How kind it was of Jesus to shed his blood for us! We ought never to forget his kindness.

Now count how many plagues God had sent Pharaoh and the people of Egypt.

1. Water turned into blood.
2. Frogs.
3. Small insects from the dust.
4. Flies.
5. Death of the animals.
6. Boils.
7. Hail and thunder.
8. Locusts.
9. Darkness.
10. Death of the eldest sons.

What dreadful plagues these were! But there will be much worse plagues in hell. I hope that you will obey God and not make him angry with you. You know why God does not send us such dreadful plagues now. Jesus is praying for us and God is waiting that we may repent.[2]

Questions for Chapter 24

When the storm came how did some people escape being hurt?

What are locusts?

When the three days' darkness came where was it light?

When Pharaoh wanted the plagues to be taken away who asked God to take them away?

What was the last plague?

Why did the Israelites mark their doors with blood?

What were they doing when Pharaoh sent them away?

Why did God desire the Israelites to eat a lamb in the night every year?

What was that supper called?

Why was it called the Passover?

Why was the lamb of the Passover like Jesus?

Can you repeat the ten plagues?

Is there any place where there are worse plagues than those ten plagues?

Scripture Verse

How terrible God is to the wicked.

'It is a fearful thing to fall into the hands of the living God.' - (Heb. 10:31).

Notes for Chapter 24

[1] The word "borrow" might equally well be translated "ask for" according to the testimony of the best commentators.

[2] 2 Pet. 3:9.

CHAPTER   25
MOSES AND THE   RED   SEA
Exod. 13:20; 14; 15:22.

The children of Israel had begun their journey to Canaan. But they had to travel a long way before they could reach that pleasant place. How could they find their way?

God himself showed them the way. He went before them in a dark cloud. The cloud moved and they moved after it. But a black cloud could not be seen at night so at night God made the cloud shine like fire. In the day the cloud was like a shade from the sun and in the night the fire gave light to the Israelites.[1] When the cloud or the fire stopped Moses commanded all the people to set up their tents on the ground. This was called "encamping".

And as soon as the cloud moved the people folded up their tents, placed them on the backs of their camels and donkeys and went on their journey.

The children of Israel went very fast till they came to the seaside. Then the cloud stopped and they set up their tents close by the sea. The sea was called the Red Sea. Perhaps you think that the water of this sea was red like blood but the water was like any other water though it was called the Red Sea.

They had not been long in their tents before they heard a great noise; it was a noise of wheels and a noise of horses. They looked and saw, far away, Pharaoh and a number of soldiers in chariots and on horses. Pharaoh had been sorry that he had let them go and he was coming after them to bring them back.

The Israelites were very frightened.

What could they do? They could not get over the sea because they had no ships but if they stayed where they were Pharaoh and his men would soon overtake them and fight against them - Pharaoh's men could fight far better than they could. What could they do? They cried to God to help them. This was right but they did something else that was not right - they began to speak angrily to Moses. "Why have you brought us up out of Egypt? We would rather have died there than come here for we shall certainly be killed."

It was ungrateful to say this to Moses but he answered them quietly, "Do not be afraid. God will fight for you and you will never see the faces of Pharaoh and his men again."

Then Moses went and prayed to God because Moses knew that God would save the children of Israel. Then God said to Moses, "Lift up your rod over the sea and I will make a dry path for the Israelites to walk upon."

So Moses lifted up his rod and the waters obeyed him. Part of the waters was lifted up on one side and part on the other. It appeared to be like two walls of water with a dry path in between. The Israelites and all their cattle walked along this path. It was the evening when they began to cross the sea and although they were walking across all the night it was not dark.

I will tell you why it was not dark. You know that the cloud in the sky shone brightly in the night and gave light to the Israelites. But God did not choose that Pharaoh should see the light so God made the black cloud move backward and it stood in the sky between the Israelites and Pharaoh. The bright side was turned towards the Israelites and the dark side towards Pharaoh, so the Israelites saw a bright light but the armies of Pharaoh were in the dark. They could not go fast because it was so dark but the Israelites walked quickly along the dry path and by the morning they got to the land that was on the other side of the sea. They had not yet got to Canaan but they had got over the sea and they were on their journey to Canaan.

Now I will tell you whether Pharaoh and his men got over the sea or not. When they came to the edge of the sea, they saw a dry path through the sea and the walls of water on each side so they went along the dry path. When they had gone about half way across the sea and were hoping soon to overtake the Israelites, God looked at them through his cloud. Pharaoh and his men heard dreadful noises and they were very frightened. It was God who made them afraid.

They could not make their chariots go on and they thought that God was going to help the Israelites to kill them so they said to each other, "Let us turn back."

Ah! It was now too late. God was going to destroy those wicked men. They drove as fast as they could that they might get out of the water but it was too late. The walls of water fell down and covered them all and they lay like stones at the bottom of the sea.

This was the end of Pharaoh and of his wicked servants. The Israelites had got safely over to the other side of the sea. As soon as they had got over God commanded Moses to lift up his rod and to make the walls of water fall down and cover the dry path. Moses had done as God told him and so the Egyptians, who were in the middle of the sea, were drowned.

In the morning the Israelites heard no sound of chariot-wheels coming after them but they saw some of the dead bodies of Pharaoh's men lying on the edge of the sea because the sea, which moves up and down, had tossed them upon the land.

Now the Israelites saw that the cruel men couldn't hurt them anymore. God had punished them for their wickedness and had saved the poor children of Abraham as he had promised.

This was a happy morning for the Israelites. They thanked

God for his goodness in saving them and they sang together a beautiful song of praise.

The song began with these words: "I will sing to the Lord because he has triumphed gloriously. He has thrown the horse and it's rider into the sea." The sea was called the "Red Sea".

The women made music and sang these same words. Moses' sister Miriam, who had watched him when a baby, played the music and the women sang with her.

How pleasant it must have been to have seen the poor Israelites singing and rejoicing! A little while before they had been working hard in the sun, they had been beaten by cruel men and had cried and groaned. Now they were slaves no more but they were on their way to a good land where they might live happily.

There is a sweeter land than Canaan. I hope we shall live there some day. Should we not praise God for telling us how we may get to that land? God will help you to get there if you ask him very often. Satan, you know, is trying to get your souls but God is stronger than Satan. God did not let Pharaoh hurt the Israelites and God can prevent Satan hurting you.[2]

Questions for Chapter 25

How did the Israelites know which was the way to Canaan?
Who tried to overtake the Israelites after they had left Canaan?
How did they cross the Red Sea?
Why could the Israelites see their way clearly in the night?
Why couldn't Pharaoh and his men see very well?
Why were Pharaoh and his men frightened when they were in the middle of the sea?
What became of Pharaoh and his men?
What did the sea toss up the next morning on the side of the sea where the Israelites were?

How did the Israelites show that they were thankful to God for saving them?

Who wishes to keep our souls from going to heaven?

Scripture Verse
How God destroyed Pharaoh and his servants.
'Thou didst blow with thy wind, the sea covered them; they sank as lead in the mighty waters.' - (Exod.15:10).

Notes for Chapter 25
[1.] Ps. 105:39.   [2.] Rom. 16:20.

* * * * * * * * * *

CHAPTER 26
MOSES, THE MANNA AND THE ROCK
Exod. 16; 17:1-7.

The children of Israel were very glad that they had got away from their cruel masters. Now they had no work to do and they had a kind master, even Moses. Ought they not to be good and happy?

They were now in a very large wilderness. I will tell you what sort of a place this wilderness was. There were hardly any men or houses but wild animals. There were snakes which bite and scorpions which sting. There were no rivers or brooks but high hills and dark pits. There were scarcely any fruit trees or corn-fields, so that there was very little to eat: and the Israelites could not sow corn nor plant fruit trees, because they were travelling. What could the poor Israelites do for food?

There were such a number of people that they wanted a great deal of food to feed them. They had taken a little bread with them in their bags when they had left Egypt but they ate it up very soon.

What should they do now? They should to pray to God. He loved them and would not let them starve. But these naughty Israelites began to grumble. They went to Moses and Aaron and said, "We wish we had died in Egypt. At least we had bread and meat there as much as we could eat but now we shall be starved. You have only brought us out of Egypt to kill us."

How ungrateful they were to Moses and to God!

Yet Moses did not answer roughly. He knew that God heard their wicked words and God did hear them. God called to Moses and said, "I have heard them and I will feed them."

Did they deserve to be fed? Oh, no! How do you think God would feed them? He would rain down bread from heaven. Wasn't this kind?

Next morning when the children of Israel looked out at their tent-doors, they saw that the ground was white. They looked to see what made the ground white and they saw little round white things on the ground. They said to each other, "What can this be? We never saw anything like it before."

Then Moses said, "This is the bread that God has sent you from heaven; gather it and take it to your tents."

So all the men got jugs and baskets and gathered the manna for themselves because their wives and for their little children. There was enough for them all; not too much, not too little but just enough. They tasted it and found it was as sweet as honey and they called it "manna".

Then they took it home and their wives cooked it for dinner; they crumbled it , baked it and made it into cakes.[1] They had manna for breakfast because dinner and for supper. Nothing but manna. It was very nice and wholesome. It was more fit for angels than for men to eat because it came from heaven[2] and did not grow out of the ground as corn does. God sent it very early, before it was light and everyone was obliged to get up early to gather it because when the sun was hot it melted away. If the Israelites did not get up early they had no food.

Moses said to them, "Do not save any of the manna because God will send you some every day. If it is all gone at night, do not be afraid; trust God. He will send you more."

But some of the people chose to save some of the manna. They were disobedient and ungrateful. They looked at their manna next morning but it was full of worms. They could not eat it but were obliged to throw it away. How foolish it is not to obey what God says!

Soon afterwards the people had no water to drink. There was no river in the wilderness and very few wells or ponds. Do you think God would let them die of thirst?

These naughty Israelites thought God would. So they went to Moses and spoke very angrily.

"Why did you bring us up out of Egypt? You mean to kill us and our little children and our cattle with thirst."

They were so angry that Moses thought they would soon throw great stones at him and kill him. Yet Moses did not answer but began to pray to God. "What shall I do for these people?" said Moses.

Then God said to Moses, "Take your rod and go up a hill and let some of the people go with you. Then, when you are come to a high place close by the rock, strike the rock and the water shall come out."

So Moses took some people with him and struck the rock and the water came running out.

A rock is a hard dry place yet God made water come out of it. The water came running down. The people at the bottom of the hill saw the water running down like a river and flowing upon the dry ground.

What a pleasant sight for the thirsty people! Their mouths were dry, their tongues were stiff and their throats burning but now they could stoop down and drink or fill their jugs with water. The poor cows, sheep and donkeys ran to the water to drink. You see how kind God had been to the people in their distress. Shouldn't they trust him always - to feel sure that he would help them?

God is very kind to you. You should never grumble like the Israelites but thank and praise God.

Questions for Chapter 26

What sort of place was the wilderness?
How did the Israelites behave when they had nothing to eat?
How did God feed them?
Why were the Israelites obliged to pick up the manna very early?
What became of the manna if it was kept to the next day?
How did the Israelites behave when they had nothing to drink?
How did God give them water?

Scripture Verse

How God relieved the thirsty Israelites.
'He clave the rocks in the wilderness and gave them drink as out of the great depths.' - (Ps. 78:15).

Notes for Chapter 26

[1] Num. 11:8. [2] Ps. 78:24, 25.

CHAPTER 27
MOSES AND MOUNT SINAI
Exod. 19; 24; 31:18.

The Israelites went on travelling through the wilderness. The wilderness was very large and it would be a long time before the people could get to Canaan.

They soon came to a very high mountain. It was called Mount Sinai. It was the same mountain where Moses had seen the bush on fire when he was keeping his sheep. Now he had brought the children of Israel to that very place where God had spoken to him first.

The Israelites placed their tents near the bottom of the mountain, for the cloud had stopped and so the Israelites knew that they ought to wait in that place.

God told Moses to come up to the top of the mountain because he had something to say to him. So Moses went up. Then God said to him, "You see how kind I have been to the children of Israel in bringing them out of Egypt. Go down and ask them whether they will do what I tell them because if they will they shall always be my own dear people.

So Moses went down and asked them if they would obey God. And they said, "Yes, we will do all that the Lord tells us."

Then Moses went up to the top of the mountain again and told God what the people had said. "They say that they will do all that you command us."

Then God said, "I am now going to let the people hear my voice and they shall see me speaking to you, Moses. Go down and tell them to get ready."

So Moses went down and said, "In three days you will

hear God's voice and see him in a cloud at the top of the mount. Get ready and wash your clothes."

So the people washed their clothes that they might all stand in clean white clothes before the Lord. Moses commanded men to put rails all round the mountain so that no one might go up to it or even touch it. Not even the sheep were to eat the grass upon that mountain for it was the mountain of God.

What a dreadful sight they saw! The mountain shaking and moving up and down. On the top a great fire was seen and a thick cloud and such a smoke went up as filled the sky with blackness and darkness. There was thunder and lightning and a sound came out of the fire. It was like the sound of a trumpet and every moment it grew louder and louder. Even Moses himself was frightened and said, "I tremble and am afraid."[1]

The Lord said to Moses, "Come up to me on the top of the mount."

So Moses went up and all the people saw him go. He went up on the shaking mount and into the midst of the smoke.

When Moses came up, God said to him (but God did not speak very loud), "Go, tell the people not to come up after you because they must not come up this mountain."

And Moses said, "I have put rails round the mount."

But still God said, "Go and tell them not to come near," because God knew how bold and disobedient the people were.

So Moses went down and said, "Do not dare to touch the mountain or you will be killed."

Then God spoke very loud indeed so that all the people heard and as they heard they trembled. Could you have seen that mountain, you would not wonder that they trembled as they stood round it.

What did God say in that loud voice? You have often heard the words at church; "These are the words that God said, "I am the Lord your God, who has brought you out of the land of

Egypt, out of the house of bondage (*or from the place where
you were slaves*).

1. You shall have no other gods before me.
2. You shall not make images and worship them (*such images
are called idols*).
3. You shall not take the name of the Lord your God in vain.
4. Remember the Sabbath day to keep it holy because on the
seventh day God rested from his work.
5. Honour your father and your mother.
6. You shall not kill.
7. You shall not commit adultery (*that is, a man must not
take away another man's wife, nor must a woman go away
from her husband and have another husband*).
8. You shall not steal.
9. You shall not bear false witness against your neighbour (*that
is, no one may tell lies of other people).*
10. You shall not covet (*or wish for other people's things*)."''

This was what God said on the mount and then he said no
more. The people were glad when God had finished speaking
because they could not bear the sound of that awesome voice
but while he was speaking they had gone farther and farther
away.

Soon they came to Moses and they said to him, "Ask God
never to let us hear his voice again, it frightens us so much. We
wish God to tell everything to you, Moses and you can tell us
what he says."

So Moses went up again to the dark cloud at the top of the
mount and told God what the people had said. "They do not
wish to hear you speak to them again," said Moses.

And God said, "They have done well in not wishing to hear

my voice. I shall speak to you and you shall tell them and oh, that they would obey me and that I might bless them always!"[2]

You see that God wanted the people to be good and happy but he knew that they did not love him in their hearts.

Moses did really love God. God talked to him a great deal. God told Moses to come up to him alone and to stay with him at the top of the mountain. So Moses stayed with God forty days and forty nights and all that time he neither ate bread nor drank water but God kept him alive and talked to him out of the thick cloud.

At the end of the time God gave Moses a book. What kind of book? It was not made of paper like the books you have seen. It was made of stone. It had only two leaves and on those leaves very little writing. God had made this stone book and God had written in it with his own finger.

You would like to know what was written in it. God had written in it all the words he had spoken in the loud voice from the cloud. The ten things God had told the Israelites are called the Ten Commandments.

He had written them down that Moses might read them to the children of Israel so that they might never forget God's commandments.

Neither ought we to forget God's commandments. They are written up in our churches so that we may read them. Did you ever see them? I should like you to learn these commandments and I will tell you the meaning of them over again.

One of these commandments was, "You shall have no other gods but me". God wanted the Israelites to love him better than anything else. But they did not. We shall hear of their wickedness. We ought to love God better than everything else for there is no one so kind and so good as God.

Questions for Chapter 27

Whom did God desire to come up the mountain that he might speak to him?

Why were rails put round the mountain?

What was seen on the mountain when God came down upon it?

What words did the people hear God say in a very loud voice?

Why did the people wish never to hear that voice again?

How long did Moses stay on the mountain alone with God?

What did God give to Moses when he had finished talking with him?

Scripture Verse

What God wanted the Israelites to do.

'O that there were such an heart in them, that they would fear me and keep all my commandments always, that it might be well with them and with their children for ever!' - (Deut. 5:29).

Notes for Chapter 27

[1.] Heb. 12:21. [2.] Deut. 5:22-29.

* * * * * * * * * *

CHAPTER 28
MOSES AND THE GOLDEN CALF
Exod. 32.

Moses stayed on the Mount forty days and forty nights. How did the Israelites behave when he was gone?

At first they behaved well but eventually they grew tired of waiting and grew impatient. They wanted to go on to Canaan quickly but the cloud stopped at the top of the mountain. They were not allowed to go on unless it moved and unless Moses told them to move. Now Moses was on the top of the mountain and they began to think he would never come back. So they went to Aaron and said to him, "Make us some gods to go before us for we do not know what has happened to Moses."

What a wicked thing to ask! But you know they had lived in Egypt, where they had seen people worship idols and they had learned to do the same.

Aaron was afraid that they would kill him if he did not make an image to please them. So he said, "Bring me your gold earrings." And the people brought him their gold earrings.

How did they get so many golden things? The women of Egypt had given them gold before they set out on their journey.

Aaron melted all their earrings in the fire then, when the gold was soft, he took a knife and cut it into an image. He made it in the shape of a calf. The people in Egypt worshipped calves.

As soon as the Israelites saw it they began to praise it and say, "This is he who brought us out of Egypt." Then Aaron put it on a high place and built an altar before it and said that they would have a great feast the next day.

The next day they rose up early. They spent the day in worshipping the calf. They took their lambs and goats and offered them on the altar of sacrifices to the calf and then rose up to sing and dance, all the while praising the calf.

You remember that they had promised a little while ago always to obey God but they did not keep their promise. One of the ten commandments was, "You shall not make an image and bow down to it." How soon they broke that commandment!

Moses was at the top of the Mount talking with God. He did not know what they were doing but God knew and he said to Moses, "Go down. The people you brought out of Egypt have made a golden calf and are worshipping it. I am very angry with them and I will kill them all but I will save you, Moses and your children."

Moses was grieved to hear that the Lord was angry and he pleaded with God to forgive the people. "Remember," he said, "how you brought them out of Egypt and how you promised Abraham that you would bless his children." The Lord heard Moses' prayer and decided that he would not kill them all. How kind Moses was to pray for the people! How kind God was to say that he would not kill all the people!

Then Moses went quickly down the mount with the book of stone in his hand. When he had almost come to the bottom of the mount he heard the noise of singing and he knew that it was the Israelites praising their calf. Eventually, he came to the tents and he saw the calf and the people dancing round it like mad or drunken people. It was a dreadful sight for Moses to see. He grew more angry still and he threw down the stone book upon the ground and broke it into pieces. The Israelites had broken God's laws and Moses broke the book in his anger and grief. Moses would not give that stone book to those people.

Do you not think the people must have been afraid when they saw Moses again?

They had thought they should never see him again but he had caught them in their wickedness.

He took the calf (and no one tried to hinder him) and threw it again in the fire. Afterwards he ground it into powder and threw it into some water and he made the Israelites drink that bitter water.

Moses was very angry with Aaron for having made the calf. Moses said to him, "Why did you let the people be so wicked?"

Aaron said, "Do not be angry with me; the people chose to

be wicked and they asked me to make a calf. I did it to please them."

This was a bad excuse. It was very wicked of Aaron to make the calf. We should not do wicked things, even when people ask us.

Moses told some of the men to take swords and to kill many people and they killed three thousand men with swords. And God made many other people fall very ill. These were the punishments that God sent to the wicked Israelites. They deserved to be killed for worshipping the golden calf but God listened to Moses' prayer and did not kill them all.

You have heard how the stone book was broken. God did not make a new one himself. He told Moses to make a book of stone and then God wrote the ten commandments in it, as he had done in the other book.

God called Moses up on to the mountain again and then God wrote the ten commandments in the stone book. God told Moses to stay with him alone on the mountain forty days and forty nights. God talked to Moses as friends talk to one another. He did not speak in that loud voice which had frightened the Israelites, nor did he make thunder, lightening and smoke when he talked to Moses. Moses liked being with God upon the mountain. Why wasn't Moses afraid of God? Because God's Spirit was in him. You will love God like a father if God's Holy Spirit is in you. God let Moses see some of his glorious brightness but God would not let him see his face because Moses would have died had he seen God's face. The angels and the people in heaven[1] see God's face but men upon earth could not bear such brightness.

I will tell you soon what God said to Moses when he was alone with him on the mountain.

Moses ate no bread and drank no water while he was alone with God.

Eventually, Moses came down again to the people with the stone book in his hand. This time the Israelites were not worshipping an image. They came up to Moses to speak to him but when they looked at his face they were afraid to come near him, even Aaron, Moses' brother, was afraid. What could the reason be?

The reason was, Moses' face shone like the sun and they could not bear such brightness. And what made his face shine?

He had been talking with God and looking upon his glory and this had made his face so bright. For God is brighter than the sun and the angels who look upon God are bright like him.

Whenever Moses talked with God his face shone for a long time afterwards. When he had done talking he wore a thick veil over his face.

I hope that your faces will one day shine bright in heaven.[2] If you love God now I am sure one day you will see him in heaven and then you will be like the angels.

Questions for Chapter 28

What did the Israelites do when they were tired of waiting for Moses?

Who made the calf?

Who told Moses what the Israelites were doing?

Who begged God not to kill them?

Why did Moses throw down the tables of stone?

What did Moses do with the calf?

What did he ask some of the people to do with their swords?

Did God give the people any other punishment?

When Moses stayed with God on the mountain forty days more, what glorious sight did God show him?

Why were the Israelites afraid to come near him when he came down again?

Why was his face bright?

When do you hope to shine as Moses did?

Scripture Verse

How the Israelites behaved to God.

'They forgot God their Saviour, which had done great things in Egypt.' - (Ps. 106:21).

Notes for Chapter 28

[1] Rev. 22:4.   [2] Dan. 12:3.

* * * * * * * * * *

CHAPTER 29
MOSES AND THE TABERNACLE
Exod. 35; 36; 37.

Moses had been with God upon the Mount a good many days. I have told you what God was teaching him but now you shall hear. God was showing him how to make a beautiful house.

Whose house was it to be? The house of God. God did not need a house because his throne is in the sky but he was so kind as to say that he would let the Israelites make him a house in the wilderness.

When Moses came down from the Mount he called all the people around him. He wanted to speak to them.

He said first, "God commands you to do no work on the Sabbath-day but to worship him and he is going to have a beautiful house made where you can come and pray to him. Who will bring me things with which to make the house?"

Had the children of Israel any beautiful things that they could bring to Moses?

You remember that the women of Egypt had given them a great deal of gold and silver, cloth and linen. They had made a calf with some of their gold but they had a great deal more besides.

But do you think they would give these things to God? Or, would they say, "We cannot spare our things. We intend to make fine clothes and to make our tents look pretty inside?" Do you think they would part with their pretty things! Yes, they would. They all went to their tents after Moses had spoken to them. They opened their boxes and their baskets, they took out gold and silver rings and earrings and beautiful pieces of cloth. Some were blue, some were purple and some were red. There was a great deal of fine white linen and skins of sheep and goats as well as beautiful kinds of wood. They brought all these things to Moses. What a large heap there must have been!

Some of the rich men had beautiful shining stones, sweet spices and oil and they brought them to Moses.

Moses was pleased to see that the people would give their things to God and most of all, he was glad that they liked to give them. They did not feel sorry when they gave them but they were glad that they had something to give. If we feel sorry when we give things, God is not pleased.[1]

Who was to make the beautiful house? It was very hard to make such a beautiful house as God would choose to have.

Moses called the children of Israel and said, "God has made two men very clever in cutting stones, in carving wood and in making all kinds of curious things and he has told me their names.

Then Moses called these two men and he gave them all the beautiful things and said, "Now begin to make the house and I will tell you what you shall make." And Moses called every one to help them and he told the two clever men to teach the others.

It is God who makes people clever so that when people can make beautiful things they should not be proud but they should thank God.

So all the people began to work. The women spun blue, purple and red thread and twisted the yarn. The men made the thread into linen and cloth. They cut the wood with saws and hammers, melted the gold and silver in the fire and then made altars, candlesticks, shovels, tongs, basins and many other things. They worked hard for many months till all the things were finished.

I will now tell you what sort of a house God had told Moses to make.

It was not a house made of bricks or stone because this house was to be moved from one place to another. So it was not fastened to the ground but was made like a tent and could be moved very easily.

You never saw so large a tent as this tent was. It was as big as a very large room. It was called "The Tabernacle."

There were many boards that were placed upright on the ground and close together.[2] These boards were the walls of the house but there were no boards at the top. Curtains were thrown over the house to cover the top. There was no door to the house but a curtain hung down in front and that curtain was instead of a door.

There was no floor to the house; green grass was the only floor.

The house was very beautiful; for the boards were covered with gold and the curtains were blue, purple and red and there were five posts of gold in front, over which a curtain hung down for the door, of which I told you before.

The house had two rooms inside. The first room was the

largest. I will tell you about the beautiful things that were placed in it.

In the first room there were three very beautiful things.

1. In the middle there was an altar of gold but no lambs were burned upon it, only sweet spices, which made the tabernacle smell most sweet. The burning spices were called "incense".

2. On one side there was a golden table and on the table twelve loaves. They were called the shew-bread, or holy bread. There was fresh bread put there every Sabbath-day.

3. On the other side there was a golden candlestick with seven lamps. There was no window in the tabernacle but these lamps made it light.

This room was very beautiful but there was another room still more beautiful.

It was the inner room on the other side of the curtain. There was a curtain between the big room and the little room. This curtain was instead of a door. It was called "The Veil".

In the little room there was a golden box, with golden angels on the top. This box was called "The Ark." Inside the box the book of stone was placed. But what made this room so glorious was that God used to come down in his cloud and fill this little room with his brightness.

The cloud rested between the golden angels on the top of the box.

The top of the box was called the mercy-seat because God sat there and God is full of love and mercy. This little room was called "The Holy of Holies".

It had no window in it and no candle but yet it was light. The glory of God made it light for God, you know, is brighter than the sun. What a place this little room must have been! It makes me think of heaven because there God lives and there He shines. But heaven is not a little place. It is a very large place and it will hold all the people who have loved God on earth, besides all the angels.

I will not tell you any more about the tabernacle now but I will write down the names of the things in the tabernacle. Can you remember what they were? In the first room, 1. the golden altar, 2. the table of shew-bread, 3. the golden candlestick. In the little room, or Holy of Holies was the Ark.

Questions for Chapter 29

When Moses was on the top of the mountain, what did God tell Moses to make?

What did the Israelites give to Moses to make the house of?

How did two men know how to make so beautiful a house?

Why wasn't this house fastened to the ground?

What was this house called?

What were the walls of the house made of?

What was thrown over the top of the house?

What kind of a door was there?

How many rooms were there in the tabernacle?

Tell me the three things in the first room?

What was burned on the golden altar?

What was placed on the golden table?

How many lamps were there in the candlestick?

What was the little room called?

What was there in it?

What was inside the ark?

What was the top of the ark called?

Where did the cloud of God sit in this little room?

What made this room light?

What made the other room light?

What makes heaven light?

Scripture Verse

About the glorious light of heaven.
'And there shall be no night there and they need no candle, neither light of the sun; for the Lord God giveth them light...' - (Rev. 22:5).

Notes for Chapter 29

[1.] 2 Cor. 9:7.
[2.] The mode of joining the boards may be explained to some children. Rings were placed in the boards and long poles were slung through these rings.

* * * * * * * * * *

CHAPTER 30
MOSES AND THE PRIESTHOOD
Exod. 38; 39; 40.

I have told you what kind of a place the tabernacle was. I am now going to tell you of some things that were placed outside of it. You know that houses often have a garden round them. The tabernacle had no garden round it but there was a large piece of ground near it, called the court, and there were posts round the court. These posts were placed at a little distance from each other and curtains were hung between the posts so there was a wall of curtains round the tabernacle.

In this court there were two things of which I shall speak to you.

1. A brass altar.

This altar was very large. It was not like the little altar of gold inside the tabernacle. This altar was not for the burning of spices but for the burning of animals, such as sheep, goats, bulls and calves. You know that God had commanded people to offer animals to him as sacrifices. Do you remember the reason? What promise had God made a long, long time before? He had promised to send his Son to die for men. God wanted people always to remember this promise so he told them to kill animals, to sprinkle their blood and to burn their bodies. Abel, Noah and Abraham offered sacrifices.

This brass altar was for the sacrifices.

The lamb was to be killed and its blood would flow all round the altar and the smoke of the burning would go up to the sky.

2. A brass basin was placed in the court.

It was very large and it was filled with water for people to wash in. I shall soon tell you who washed in this basin.

Who was to offer the sacrifices? Aaron. God said that Aaron should be the "High Priest". Aaron was to offer the sacrifices, to burn the incense and to light the lamps of the candlestick.

God said that Aaron might go into the little room, the Holy of Holies. God would not allow any person but Aaron to go in there and he only allowed him to go in once every year. Aaron was allowed lift up the veil and see the cloud upon the mercy-seat. Moses was also allowed to go in and God promised to speak to him in that little room.[1]

I am glad that there is a brighter place where we may go one day and hear God speak to us.

God commanded Moses to have some beautiful clothes made for Aaron to wear. The two clever men, of whom I told you before, knew how to make them.

Aarons cloths:

1. He was to wear a white dress with long sleeves.

2. A blue robe. He was to wear this over the white dress. Little golden bells were hung round the edge of it and they would sound sweetly as Aaron moved along.

3. An ephod made of white linen, worked all over with

purple, scarlet and gold. Aaron was to wear the ephod over the blue robe.

4. A band round his waist, called a girdle. It was made of white linen and was worked with purple, red thread and gold wire.

5. A breastplate. Aaron was to wear this in front. It was made of linen covered with twelve shining stones. It was to be fastened to Aaron's shoulders by gold chains.

6. A mitre. Aaron was to wear a high white cap upon his head, called a mitre. "Holiness to God" was written on it in gold. Aaron ought to be holy because he was to offer sacrifices to God.

Aaron was to wear no shoes upon his feet but he was often to wash his feet and his hands at the brass basin.[2]

Aaron had four sons. God said that they should help him to offer sacrifices. Aaron's sons were to wear white clothes but not the same beautiful clothes as Aaron. They were to be called "Priests," and Aaron was to be called "High Priest."

It was a long time before the tabernacle was made. Although all the people worked very hard yet the things were not finished for almost a year.

God commanded Moses to set up the tabernacle.

Moses set up the boards for the walls of the tabernacle and covered the top with curtains. He placed the ark in the Holy of Holies and he put the table, the candlestick and the golden altar in the largest room. He set up the posts and the curtains all around the court and put the brass altar and basin in it. Then Moses poured oil upon all the things; this pouring of oil was called "anointing".

Then Moses put upon Aaron his beautiful robes and put the white clothes upon their heads and so anointed them.

Then God came down in his cloud and his brightness filled the whole place and so his presence was there.

Was it not pleasant for the Israelites to think that God lived in a house among them? The cloud could be seen outside the tabernacle as well as inside and in the night it shone like fire. How kind it was of God to let the people see some of his brightness! God wanted them to be very good and to obey all he said. God is very near to us, too, though we cannot see him but we hope to see him some day.

What place is much more beautiful than the tabernacle was? Heaven. If we get to heaven we shall be much more glorious than Aaron was and we shall see God's face forever and ever and so we shall be quite happy.

THE HIGH PRIEST'S DRESS.

1. The white coat, with long sleeves.
2. The blue robe.
3. The ephod.
4. The girdle.
5. The breastplate.
6. The mitre.

Questions for Chapter 30

What was placed round the court of the tabernacle?
What two things were placed in the court?
What was to be burned upon the altar of brass?
Who was to wash in the brass basin?
Who was to be the high priest?
Where might the high priest go only once a year?
What clothes was Aaron to wear?
What was to be written on Aaron's mitre?
Who was to help Aaron to offer sacrifices?
What sort of clothes were they to wear?
Who set up the tabernacle?

On what did Moses pour oil?
What was this pouring of oil called?
What was seen upon the tabernacle after it was set up?
Why ought the Israelites to have been very happy?

Scripture Verse

Where God promised to dwell.
'And I will dwell among the children of Israel and will be their
God.' - (Exod. 29:45).

Notes for Chapter 30

[1.] Exod. 25:22. Also Num. 7:89.

[2.] The water came pouring out of the basin through little holes, as
water comes out of a spout and the priests held their hands and feet
under the water as it was falling.

* * * * * * * * * *

CHAPTER 31
MOSES AND THE JOURNEY OF THE ISRAELITES

Now the Israelites had a place in which to worship God
and to offer sacrifices.

Every morning the priests offered up a lamb on the brass
altar[1] and burned incense on the golden altar in the tabernacle.[2]
And every evening they offered another lamb and burned some
more incense.

God sent some fire down from heaven to burn the sacrifices
with[3] and the priests never let the fire go out. The priests always
kept the lamps burning in the tabernacle. Every Sabbath day
the priests placed some fresh bread on the golden table and
when they put the fresh bread on it they took away the old
bread and ate it themselves.[4]

The people went into the great court of the tabernacle to worship God and to see the lamb killed and burned on the altar. Afterwards they saw Aaron go into the tabernacle to burn incense. The people stood in the court while Aaron was in the tabernacle praying for them. They waited till he came out again to bless them. He lifted up his hands and said, "The Lord bless you and keep you."[5]

Who prays for us in heaven? Who will come one day and bless us?[6] The Lord Jesus Christ. He is our High Priest.

While the people had been making the tabernacle they had stayed in one place near the great mount Sinai but soon after it was finished the cloud of God moved. Then the priests blew two silver trumpets.

Why did they blow these trumpets? To tell the people that they were to move to another place.

Then the people packed up their tents and furniture and put them on the backs of their camels and donkeys. Then the priests went into the tabernacle and covered all the things in it with blue cloths. No one was allowed to look while they were covering the things. Then they gave them to some men to carry upon their shoulders[7] but they covered the ark with the beautiful veil and they carried it themselves.[8] There were two long golden sticks fastened to it. The priests held the ends of the sticks and so they carried it.

Then the priests instructed some men to carry the curtains and the posts and the boards of the tabernacle.[9] The priests went first[10] with the ark and all the people followed them and God, in the cloud, showed them the way. When the cloud stopped the priests and the people stopped and set up the tabernacle and the tents.[11] In this manner the Israelites travelled all through the wilderness.

What a happy people they were, to have such a God to show them the way to Canaan! They ought always to have been praising him for his goodness. He fed them with manna and gave them water from the rock and he had promised to bring them to a goodland. Besides all this he had promised to send his Son to die for them and the lambs were killed, you know, to make them remember that promise.

I hope we shall not forget how Jesus died upon the cross. And I hope we shall get to that good land, called heaven. God wishes us to get there and Jesus Christ is praying for us.

Questions for Chapter 31

What sacrifice was offered every morning and every evening on the brass altar?
What was it the priests never let go out?
Who ate the shew-bread when it was taken from the golden table?
Who was allowed to go into the tabernacle?
Who is our high priest? What is he doing for us in heaven?
When did the priests blow the silver trumpets?
Who carried the ark?
What good land do we hope to reach?

Scripture Verse

About the Lamb who died for us.
'...Behold the Lamb of God, which taketh away the sin of the world.' - (John 1:29).

Notes for Chapter 31

1. Exod. 29:38-42.   2. Exod. 30:7,8.   3. Lev. 9:24.
4. Lev. 24:5-9.   5. Num. 6:23 to end.   6. Acts 3:26.
7. Num. 4:5-15.   8. Deut. 31:9.   9. Num. 4:23-33.
10. Num. 10:33.   11. Num. 9:15 to end.

SECTION 3

NUMBERS

Introduction

Exodus ends with the Israelites camping in the Desert of Sinai after receiving God's Law. It has been a little over a year since they came out of Egypt and the book of Numbers carries on from this point. Numbers reveals a little more about God's Laws but also exposes the grumbling and doubting on the part of the Israelites when things became difficult. We learn that they were afraid of the people in the Promised Land and as a result, they had to wander around in the desert for forty years and learn a lesson about having faith in God.

Numbers takes us up to the point at which the Israelites were preparing to enter the Promised Land. Sadly, because of their grumbling nearly all the adults who had been saved from Egypt did not survive to see it. Only Caleb and Joshua remained to lead the people because they had obeyed and trusted God. In fact, Numbers reveals that just before Moses' death Joshua was chosen by God to be the new leader of the Israelites.

Some Suggestions for Study

Before each chapter, ask yourself if you have been grumbling about anything or whether you feel more like Joshua and Caleb and want to trust in God. If you have been grumbling, pray that God will encourage you to move forward in faith. And if you feel like Joshua and Caleb, give God the praise that you have been given the grace to move on.

CHAPTER 32
MOSES AND THE TWELVE SPIES
Num. 13; 14:1-40

Eventually, the Israelites came quite near the land of Canaan.

They could see the tops of the high hills that were in Canaan. They wanted to know what sort of a land it was and what sort of people lived there.

So the Israelites came to Moses and said, "We wish to send some men to look at the land and we wish them to come back and tell us what kind of a land it is."[1]

Would Moses send some men?

Moses wanted to know whether God would like some men to go.

Soon God said to Moses, "Send twelve men into Canaan to see the land." So Moses called twelve Israelites and said to them, "Go into Canaan and walk up among the high mountains and look at the land. See whether there are many people living in the land and what kind of people they are, whether they are strong or weak, whether there are many trees, much corn and grass in the land. Bring back some fruit to show us the kind of fruit that grows in the land."

So the twelve men set out on their journey. These men were called the twelve spies. They walked up and down the hills and by the side of the water. They saw gardens and some fields covered with sheep, some fields full of corn, trees laden with fruit. They saw holes in the trees which the bees had filled with honey so that the honey dropped on the ground. They saw large towns with high walls around them and they saw many strong men, some of them giants.

At last they came to a brook, or pond. A vine grew by it

and on the vine were ripe grapes - one of the bunches was very, very large. They said, "Let us bring it back to show to the children of Israel." One man could not carry this bunch by himself. So they took a staff and one man held one end of the staff and another held the other. The rest of the men picked figs and other fruit and carried them back to the tents.

The spies were forty days looking at the land of Canaan.

When they came back, the people saw the beautiful bunch of grapes. There were no such grapes in the wilderness. The spies then said, "The land of Canaan is a fine land, full of milk and honey but we cannot get into it because the people live in great towns with high walls. They are very strong and some of them are giants. When we saw them we felt as if we were like little as grasshoppers."

Then the children of Israel were very frightened and they began to murmur and to weep. "Ah!" they said, "we shall be killed if we try to get in."

It was wicked to say this because God had promised to help the Israelites to get into Canaan. It is wicked not to believe what God says.

Two of the spies were very good men. Their names were Joshua and Caleb. They did not wish to frighten the people and Caleb stood up and said, "Let us go into the land because we can conquer the people that are in it."

But the ten other spies said, "No, we cannot, because the people of Canaan are stronger than we."

These ten spies were very wicked men because they knew that God had promised to help the Israelites to conquer the men of Canaan and they ought to have told the people to trust in God.

The Israelites cried all night long. They were angry with Moses and Aaron for bringing them out of Egypt and said, "O that we had died in Egypt or in the wilderness! The people of Canaan will kill us with their swords and they will kill our wives and our little children!"

They spoke in this way all night long instead of praying to God to help them. At last they said, "Let us go back into Egypt."

They knew that Moses would not take them back. So they said, "We can make another man captain over us and he will take us back to Egypt."

Moses and Aaron heard these wicked words. They were full of grief and they fell down on the ground on their faces.

What had grieved Moses and Aaron?

They were grieved to see the people so wicked.

Then Joshua and Caleb stood up and said to the people, "We have seen the land and it is a very beautiful land. If we trust in God he will help us to fight but the people of Canaan have no God to help them. Therefore, we ought not to be afraid of them."

The children of Israel would not listen to Joshua and Caleb but were going to kill them with stones, when God shone brightly upon the tabernacle so that the people saw that he was angry.

Moses was lying on his face on the ground but God spoke to him and said, "How long will these people provoke me? I will kill them with a plague." Then Moses prayed to God for the people.

"O pardon these people," he said, "and their great sin. You have forgiven them many times and Your mercy is very great."

God heard Moses' prayer and said, "I have pardoned them. I will not kill them all now but they shall not come into Canaan; only their children shall come in. They shall stay in the wilderness forty years and they shall all die in it and when their children are grown up they shall go into the land of Canaan. But there are two of the men who shall go into Canaan. They are Caleb and Joshua."

Moses told the children of Israel what God had said. When the people heard it they were very unhappy and they murmured. The ten wicked spies soon fell sick and died but Joshua and Caleb lived still.

How sad it was for the people to think they should never see that land of Canaan but should die in the wilderness!

Yet they deserved to die because they had not believed what God had said.

God has promised to give us his Spirit if we ask him and to take us to heaven. Do you believe this promise? Then you will ask God for his Spirit. But if you do not care about heaven, then you will not pray to God for his Spirit. Then God will be angry and in the end he will say that you shall never get to heaven.[2]

Questions for Chapter 32

Why did Moses send twelve men into Canaan?

What did these men bring back with them?

What sort of a land did the spies say that Canaan was?

What sort of people did the spies say lived in Canaan?

What were the names of the two good spies?

Why ought not the Israelites to have been afraid of the people of Canaan?

What was Moses doing when God spoke to him from the tabernacle?

How did God say that he would punish the Israelites for their wickedness?

Would the little children die in the wilderness?

Would any of the grown-up people be allowed to go into Canaan?

How many years would it be before the Israelites would go into Canaan?

Scripture Verse

How the Israelites behaved when the spies came back from viewing the land.

'..They despised the pleasant land, they believed not his [God's] word but murmured in their tents and hearkened not unto the voice of the Lord.' - (Ps. 106:24, 25).

Notes for Chapter 32

[1.] Deut. 1:22.   [2.] Heb. 4:11.

* * * * * * * * * *

CHAPTER 33
THE SIN OF MOSES AND AARON
Num. 22:1-13, 22-29.

The children of Israel lived in the wilderness for many years. They moved about from place to place. One day they came to a place where there was no water. How do you think they behaved? Did they pray to God or did they murmur?

They murmured against Moses and Aaron as they always did when they were unhappy. They said, "O that we had died before this time! Why did you bring us out of Egypt into this wilderness? Here there are no figs, no grapes, no kind of nice fruit and now there is no water to drink!"

They forgot that it was because of their own wickedness that they were still in the wilderness because if they had obeyed God they would then have been sitting under their own trees, eating their own fruit in Canaan.

Moses and Aaron were very much grieved to hear them murmur. They went away from the people and fell on their faces before the tabernacle and soon God spoke to them.

He said, "Take the rod and call the people and go to the

rock and speak to it. Water shall come out of the rock and then the people and the animals shall drink."

So Moses took the rod (the rod was kept near the ark). Then Moses and Aaron called the people together and told them to look at what they were going to do.

Moses and Aaron felt very angry with the people and they said, "Hear now, you rebels!" (which means *grumblers*). "Must we fetch water for you out of this rock?"

Then Moses lifted up his hand, struck the rock twice with his rod and the water came flowing out in streams and the people and the cattle began to drink.

Do you think that Moses and Aaron had behaved right? Had God told them to strike the rock?

God had said, "Speak to the rock."

Was it right to speak so impatiently and to say, "Must we fetch water for you, you rebels?"

Moses and Aaron had let their bad tempers get the better of them. God was displeased with them.

Do you think that God would punish them? God loved Moses and Aaron yet he would punish them when they did wrong. He would forgive them and take them to heaven but he would give them some punishment.[1] You shall hear what the punishment should be.

Soon afterwards, God said to Moses and Aaron, "Because you have done this, you shall not go into Canaan. You shall die in the wilderness."

What a great punishment this was! Moses had often longed to see that land of Canaan. He had often wanted to see the Israelites happy in their own houses and gardens. He had longed to see the place where Abraham had built altars and worshipped God but now he must die in the wilderness. He prayed to God to excuse him this punishment but God would not. God said, "Ask me no more to do this." Then Moses knew that he must bear his punishment.[2]

Moses was the meekest man in all the world. The Israelites had often spoken ungratefully to him and he had made no answer. Yet in the end he himself got into a bad temper.

You see how much God hates bad temper. God wishes us to be very good tempered, like the Lord Jesus Christ, who never spoke an angry word. Are you like Him? Can you bear to be pushed and slapped and not push and slap again? If a child takes your place can you ask him gently to let you have it? And if he will not, can you take another quietly? When children call you rude names can you be gentle and not call them rude names too? A good tempered child can do all these things. God can make you very good. Will you pray to God to make you meek, like Jesus? Moses, too, was very meek though he fell into a temper once.

Was it unkind of God to punish Moses and Aaron? God cannot be unkind but he will punish people for disobedience. God wanted to show the Israelites that he would not allow any person to be disobedient, not even Moses.

At last the time came for Aaron to die for God chose Aaron to die first. God said to Moses, "Go up to the top of the hill with Aaron and take Aaron's eldest son with you. Aaron will die on the top and you must put his clothes upon his son." God chose Aaron's son to be high priest instead of Aaron, so he was to wear Aaron's clothes.

So Aaron put on his beautiful high priest's clothes; his blue robe with the golden bells and his ephod over it, his shining breastplate and his white mitre with the golden writing upon it. Then Aaron walked with Moses and his son to the top of the hill and all the people looked at them as they were walking up. Aaron knew that he should never walk down that hill but still he obeyed God and bore his punishment meekly.

When they were come to the top Moses took the beautiful clothes off his brother Aaron and put them on Aaron's son.

Moses parted from his brother Aaron on the top of that hill for there Aaron died. Moses and the son left him dead upon the top and came down the hill together. Then the people saw that Aaron was dead and that there was another high priest.

Aaron's soul went up to heaven because God had forgiven him. If he had not spoken so angrily he would have lived to see the land of Canaan. Moses knew that he should die very soon but God did not choose for him to die yet.

Questions for Chapter 33

How did the people behave when they had no water to drink?
How did God desire Moses to bring water out of the rock?
What was it Moses did instead of speaking to the rock?
What did Moses and Aaron say as they stood by the rock?
How did God say that he would punish them?
Was Moses often angry? Was Moses meek?
How would a meek child behave if he were ill-treated?
Who went with Aaron up the hill when he was to die?
What clothes did Aaron wear?
Upon whom did Moses put the clothes just before Aaron died?
Why did Moses put the clothes on Aaron's son?
Who was the high priest when Aaron was dead?

Scripture Verse

A prayer to be kept from sinful words.
'Set a watch, O Lord, before my mouth; keep the door of my lips.' - (Ps. 141:3).

Notes for Chapter 33

[1.] Ps. 99:8.   [2.] Deut. 3:23-26.

CHAPTER   34.
MOSES AND THE SERPENT OF BRASS
Num. 21:4 -9.

The children of Israel travelled in the wilderness for many years. Sometimes, when they were close to Canaan, the cloud moved the other way and the Israelites were obliged to go on travelling in the wilderness. This made them very unhappy because they longed very much to get into the land of Canaan. If they had not behaved so badly in the wilderness, they would soon have got to Canaan but God punished them by not letting them in.

How do you think they bore their punishment? You know that they were always ready to murmur. They spoke against God and against Moses. They said, "Why have you brought us out of Egypt? We shall die in the wilderness. There is no bread here, nor any water and we do not like this manna."

Was the manna nice food? It was fit for angels; spotless, white and sweet as honey. It came down from heaven and did not grow out of the ground as corn does. Yet these ungrateful Israelites said that they hated it and were tired of eating it.

God sent them a dreadful punishment this time. You know there were wild animals and horrible serpents and scorpions in the wilderness but God took care of the Israelites so that they were not hurt by them. Now God sent serpents whose mouths burned like fire. These serpents came rushing among the tents. The Israelites could not get away from them. If the Israelites climbed up in a high place, the serpents could climb after them and they could get through the smallest places.

Many, many of the Israelites were bitten by these serpents.

After they had been bitten they grew sick and were full of pain and got worse and worse till at last they died. There was no medicine that could cure these bites, no plaster could make them well. Every person who was bitten was sure to die.

The Israelites came to Moses and said, "We have sinned; we have spoken against the Lord and against you. Pray to the Lord to take the serpents from us." For the serpents were still among the tents.

Did Moses pray to God for the people or did he say, "You deserve to be punished and I will not help you"? Moses was kind and forgiving and he prayed for the people.

The Lord heard Moses' prayer and he did more than Moses asked. God not only called away the serpents but he told him how to cure the people who were bitten by the serpents.

What do you think God told Moses to do? Did he tell Moses to give them some medicine or to put a plaster on the bites? You will be surprised to hear the strange things that God told Moses to do.

He said, "Take some brass, make it into the image of a serpent, put it on a pole and tell the people who are bitten to look at it. Those who look at it shall be made well."

Was not this a strange way of making them well?

Moses believed God. He took some brass and made it soft in the fire. Then made it like one of the fiery serpents and put it on a pole, lifted it up where every one could see it and called to the sick people to look quickly at the serpent and be made well.

The people who were bitten could crawl to the door of their tents and lift up their dying eyes towards the serpent. After they had looked their pain went away. They felt well, strong and could walk and praise God.

Did all the people who were sick look at the serpent? I do not know. Perhaps some said, "How could looking at a serpent

make us well?" If there were any such people they must have
died. But I hope they all looked at the serpent.

And now, children, do you know that a serpent has bitten
us? A serpent has bitten our souls. What serpent do I mean?
That old serpent the devil. He has bitten our souls; that is, he
has made us naughty. You have heard how he made Adam
and Eve naughty in the Garden of Eden. We are naughty, too,
because we are Adam's children. Who can make our souls
better from this bite? Who can save us from dying forever and
ever? Who can give us eternal life?

The serpent of brass was lifted up on a pole - Jesus was
lifted up on the cross. Now we must look at Jesus. What do
I mean by looking at Jesus? I do not mean looking at him with
our eyes. It would not save us to see Jesus on the cross. Many
wicked people saw him die and were not saved. The "looking,"
I mean is thinking of him and loving him. When you think of
Jesus having died for you and when you love him for it, then
you look at him with your heart.

I hope that you will look at Jesus with your heart that you
might be saved from sin and Satan and hell.

Questions for Chapter 34

How did the Israelites behave when God made them stay a
long time in the wilderness?

What living creatures did God send to punish them?

What did God want Moses to do to cure the people who were
bitten?

Who has made our souls ready to die?

When did Satan first make people's souls naughty?

To whom must we look that our souls may live?

Are we to look at Jesus with the eyes of our body?

What do you mean by "looking at Jesus"?

Scripture Verse

Why the serpent of brass was like Christ.

'And as Moses lifted up the serpent in the wilderness, even so must the Son of man be lifted up: that whosoever believeth in him should not perish but have eternal life.' - (John 3:14,15).

* * * * * * * * * *

CHAPTER 35
THE DEATH OF MOSES
Deut. 31; 32; 33; 34.

The time was almost come for Moses to die. The Israelites were very soon to go into Canaan but Moses was not to go there with them.

Moses had written many books while he had been in the wilderness and now he had almost finished them. Should you like to know what Moses had written about in these books?

He had written about how God made the world, how Adam ate the fruit, how Cain killed Abel. He had written about Noah, Abraham, Isaac and Jacob. He had written about Joseph and his wicked brothers. He had written about himself, how he had been saved from the water when he was a baby. He had written about the ten plagues, the ten commandments and the tabernacle. He had written about his own sin. All I have told you Moses had written down in five books. They have all been copied in other books and we can read all Moses wrote because it is in the Bible.

But how did Moses know all these things? He was not born when God made the world. How could he write about things he never saw? Could anybody have told him how God made the world? No one was born when God made the world. No one but God could tell him and God did tell him.

God spoke to Moses by his Spirit. While Moses was writing with his pen, God was putting thoughts in his mind. So he always knew what to write.

Moses did not write in such books as you have seen. His paper was rolled up like a piece of cloth at the shop. He wrote five rolls and these he called his books. If you had read in Moses' book you would have unrolled it as you read it.

When Moses had finished writing his books he called his priests and told them to take care of his books. Moses said to them, "You must read these books to all the Israelites, to the men, the women and the little children that they may know how to please God."

Moses knew that he must soon leave the Israelites. He wanted very much that some good man should take care of them after he was dead because he loved them very much though they had behaved so badly towards him. So Moses begged God to give them into the care of some good man.[1] God heard his prayer and said to Moses, "I have found a man who will take care of the children of Israel after you are dead."

Who do you think this man was? It was Joshua, one of the good spies. He had helped Moses to do God's work for forty years[2] so that Moses had taught him a great deal. Moses was very glad that Joshua would take care of the Israelites when he was dead.

Moses called Joshua and said to him, "God will let you take the children of Israel into Canaan. You must be very brave because you will have to fight against the wicked people but God will help you, so do not be afraid. God will never leave you, nor forsake you."

Moses wanted to speak to the people before he died and advise them to be good so he called all the people together and told them he was going to die. "I am very old," he said, "I am a hundred and twenty years old this day. I offended God and I must not go into the land of Canaan but Joshua will take you there. Remember to obey God and to love him and he will always bless you but if you worship idols and are wicked God will punish you."

God told Moses to teach the people a song that they might sing it after he was dead. This song was about God's kindness to the children of Israel.

You learn songs or hymns about God. Do you know why you are taught to repeat them? It is to help you to think of God, that you may love him. Some children repeat their hymns as soon as they wake in the morning.

After Moses had taught the people the song, he blessed them and then he left them forever. God said to Moses, "Go up that high mountain alone. I cannot let you go into Canaan but I will let you see that beautiful land of Canaan from the top of that mountain."

Moses was glad that he was allowed see Canaan, though he could not go in. So Moses went up the mountain all alone. He was very old yet he was not weak. He could walk as well as when he was young and he could see as well for his eyes were not dim. He read and wrote and saw things far away. God had not let him grow weak or blind.

I think the Israelites must have felt very sad when they saw Moses go up that mountain all alone and when they knew they would see him no more. I hope they felt sorry for having behaved so ill to him and for having so provoked him at the rock. What a kind friend Moses had been to them!

When Moses was at the top of the hill he looked and saw the land of Canaan far away. It was a beautiful land and full of green hills and rivers, of fields ripe with corn and of trees laden with fruit. Moses was glad that the children of Israel would live in such a land where they could worship God.

When Moses had looked at the land, he died. No friend

was near to close his eyes or to hear his last sigh. No brother's hand was there to wrap him in his grave-clothes or to cover him with the green earth.

Would God leave Moses' body to be eaten by the wild animals to be pecked by the birds of the air? No, God himself buried Moses, not upon the top of the hill but in some secret place under the hill. No one knows where Moses lies. Only the angels who carried his soul to God because they watch over God's children in the dust. When the last trumpet sounds, Moses will rise from that grave and shine like the stars in the sky. Thus Moses died. He was the only man to whom God talked as to a friend. God spoke to Moses face to face, as friends talk to each other.

I shall tell you no more of Moses but you will see him in heaven, if you go there. You remember that he might have been a prince in the land of Egypt. King Pharaoh's daughter saved him from the water, she gave him fine things and called him her son. But Moses wanted to help the poor children of Israel and he did not choose to be a prince in Egypt.

Was it not much better that Moses should help the poor children of Israel than that he should be rich and grand? You see that God loved Moses and made him a friend and took him to heaven when he died.

Now, I hope you will be like Moses. I hope that when you are grown up you will try to help poor people and teach them about God. Think, how kind Jesus has been to you. He left heaven that he might save us and that we might know God.

Questions for Chapter 35

What did Moses write down in five books?
How did Moses know what to write?
Whom did Moses want to read his books to the Israelites?

Who was to take charge of the people when Moses was dead?
Why did God want Moses to go up to the top of a high mountain before he died?
Who buried Moses?
How did God to talk to Moses?
If you are like Moses what shall you like doing when you are grown up?

Scripture Verse

How God shows His love when people sin.
'As many as I love, I rebuke and chasten...' - (Rev. 3:19).

Notes for Chapter 35

[1.] Num. 27:15,16.   [2.] Exod. 24:13.

SECTION 4

JOSHUA

Introduction

The Book of Joshua tells us about the next stage in God's wonderful plan to save his people. It tells us of the fulfillment of part of God's promise to the Israelites and as the story unfolds, we see that He has also kept his promise to Abraham.

Joshua begins with the Israelites waiting to cross the River Jordan and step into the land that God had promised. Moses has died and the people have a new leader called Joshua. The rest of the book is an account of how God makes it possible for the Israelites to settle in the land by leading in the battles against the inhabitants.

Some Suggestions for Study

In this section, before each chapter, think about challenges that you have faced in the past and how you lived through them. Then, think of challenges now or in the future and thank God for being there to help. Pray that just as He brought down the walls of Jericho, He will help you. Find some small clean stones and have them near each time you pray to remind you of the fallen wall of Jericho and how God helped his people past this obstacle.

CHAPTER 36
JOSHUA AND RAHAB
Josh. 2.

The Israelites were now near Canaan. They were sorry that Moses was dead but Joshua was to take care of them instead of Moses. Joshua was to tell them what to do. God would speak to him and he would tell them what God said.

The Israelites would soon have to fight a great deal. Whom would they have to fight against? The wicked people who lived in Canaan. God decided that they should be killed as punishment for their wickedness and God decided that the Israelites should live in their land instead of them.

There was a great river that rolled between the wilderness and Canaan. The Israelites would be obliged to cross the river before they could get into Canaan. The Israelites could see the green hills of Canaan on the other side of the river and they also saw a great town with high walls all round it. This town was called Jericho. It was in Canaan and wicked people lived in it. The Israelites knew that they would soon have to fight against the people who lived in this town.

Joshua told two of the Israelites to go to the town, to look at it, to come back and tell him about the town and about the people who lived in it. These men were called "spies" because they were sent to spy or to look at the town.

Joshua did not wish the people of Jericho to know when these two spies came in to the town in case the wicked people should kill them. So they went to the town when it was almost dark. The spies got over the river. There was one place in the river where the water was not very deep and where people could get over. This was called a ford.

The gate of Jericho used to be shut when it was dark but the spies came just before the gate was shut. They went to the house of a woman named Rahab who kept an inn. Her house was built upon the wall of Jericho. The spies hoped that nobody had seen them come into Jericho but some people had seen them and these people went and told the king of Jericho that two Israelites were in Rahab's house. The king of Jericho knew that the Israelites meant to come and fight against him so he wanted to kill these two spies and he sent some men to Rahab's house to bring them to him.

What could the poor spies do? Where could they go? But God took care of them. He put it into Rahab's heart to be kind to them. Rahab had taken the spies, when they first came, to the top of her house to hide them. The roof of her house was not slanting like the roof of this house. It was flat, like the floor. On the roof of Rahab's house there were many stalks of flax. What is flax? Flax is a plant and the stalks of flax are made into thread. Rahab had spread the stalks upon the roof of her house to dry them. When the spies had climbed up the stairs to the top of the house she told them to lie down and she covered them all over with the stalks so that nobody could see them.

The men who had come to bring the spies to the king of Jericho could not find them in Rahab's house so they went to look for them outside the city, among the hills and by the riverside.

When the king of Jericho's men had gone Rahab crept up the stairs to speak to the spies. It was night so she could talk to them on the roof without being seen. The men came from under the heaps of flax. Rahab had been taught to worship idols but you will see that she now believed in the true God and not in idols. She had a great favour to ask of the spies. She

was very afraid that when the Israelites came over the river to
fight against Jericho, they might kill her and her friends so now
she begged the spies to promise to save her and those she
loved.

Poor Rahab said, "I know that God will let the people of
Israel come and live in Canaan. Everybody is very much
frightened in case you will kill them. We have heard how your
God helped you to pass through the Red Sea. I know that
your God is the only true God. Now promise that when you
come to this town you will not kill me, nor my father and mother
and brothers and sisters. I have been kind to you and will you
be kind to me?"

Do you think that the spies would promise to save Rahab
and her friends? O yes! How kind she had been to them in
hiding them! Besides this, Rahab feared God. The spies
promised that they would not let her be killed or her father or
mother, or brothers or sisters.

How glad Rahab must have been when they made her this
promise! There was one thing the spies instructed her not to
do; that was, not to tell anybody about their having been to
Jericho. The spies said, "If you will not tell anybody about our
having come here, we promise to save your life and the life of
your father and mother and brothers and sisters."

Then Rahab helped the spies to get out of the town. Could
the spies go out at the gates? It was night and the gates were
shut. If the spies waited till the morning the people of Jericho
would see them going out and would kill them. But Rahab
found a way of letting the spies go.

Her house was built on the wall of Jericho; one of the
windows in her house looked towards the green hills outside
of Jericho. The window was high so Rahab let the men down
out of the window by rope.

The men had said to her, "Take that red rope and bind it to

your window. Bring your father and mother, brothers and sisters into your house. If they stay in it with you, we promise that they shall not be killed when the Israelites come to fight against this town but if you or any of your relations are walking in the streets when we come then perhaps you or they may be killed. Neither may you tell any other person about our having come here; you must keep it a secret." When the spies had said this they went away and they hid themselves among the hills for three days in case the men of Jericho were watching by the river to kill them. At the end of three days they got over the river, came back to Joshua and told him all that had happened. Joshua was glad to hear that the people of Jericho were so frightened and he felt sure that God would help him to conquer all the people in Canaan.

The spies told Joshua about Rahab. They said, "You will know which house is Rahab's because she has bound a red rope to the window." Joshua commanded that nobody was to kill the people in the house with the red rope on the window.

Do you think that Rahab forgot to bind the red rope on the window? Oh, no! She bound it there and she brought her father and mother and brothers and sisters into her house and she did not tell any of the wicked people of Jericho about the spies. Nobody knew why she bound a red rope to her window.

Do you think that Rahab felt frightened now? Could she not trust the spies? Would they break their word? How Rahab must have thanked God for promising to save her when the people of Jericho would be killed!

There is a day coming when many wicked people will be killed and burned in the fire. You have heard of the judgment day. Do you not hope that God will save you in that day? Then do as Rahab did. Ask God to promise to save you. He will save you if you ask him. If you are really afraid of God, as

Rahab was, you will often pray to him to forgive you for Jesus Christ's sake.

God will hear you and he will remember his promise on the judgment day and he will not let you be hurt.

Questions for Chapter 36

What city did the Israelites see on the other side of the river?

Why did Joshua send two spies to Jericho?

To whose house did they go?

Who went to Rahab's house to look for them?

Where had Rahab hid them?

What promise did Rahab ask the spies to make to her?

How did the spies come out of Jericho?

Why did they desire Rahab to bind the red rope to her window?

In what day do you hope God will save you?

Scripture Verse

What we must now do, if we hope to be saved in the judgment-day.

'...seek righteousness, seek meekness; it may be ye shall be hid in the day of the Lord's anger.' - (Zeph. 2:3).

* * * * * * * * * *

CHAPTER 37
JOSHUA AND THE RIVER JORDAN
Josh. 3; 4; 5:1,11,12.

The people of Israel were now close to Canaan but a deep river ran between the wilderness and Canaan. It was called the river Jordan. How were the Israelites to get over it?

Could they go over in boats?

How could wood be got to make boats for so many people?

Could they make a bridge? The people in Canaan would have shot arrows at the Israelites while they were making a bridge.

Could they swim over?

How could the children and the women swim? And how could they take their tents over?

God could help them to get over. How had they got over the Red Sea?

You shall hear what God told Joshua to do.

Joshua rose up early in the morning and he said to the people, "Look and see where the priests take the ark and follow them but do not go too near."

Then Joshua said to the priests, "Take up the ark and walk on."

The ark (which was a golden box) was covered with a blue cloth, that no-one might see it or see the golden angels on the top. Two long sticks were run through the rings joined to the ark and the priests held the ends of the sticks.

The priests took up the ark when Joshua told them. They went to the edge of the water not knowing what they were to do. They were dressed in white and their feet were bare.

Joshua called to them and commanded them to stand still. Then he spoke to all the people. "Now," he said, "you will see a great wonder that God is going to do. When the priests put their feet in the water a dry path shall be made."

All the people were coming out of their tents. They had got all their things ready for their journey and were looking at the priests.

Then Joshua commanded the priests to put their feet into the water. As soon as they touched it the water stood up like a wall on one side and there was a dry path made through the river.[1] The priests walked along till they came to the middle of the river then they stopped and Joshua said to the people, "Now do you pass over Jordan."

While the people were crossing the priests stood quite still in the middle of the dried-up river. At last, all the people had got over into the land of Canaan, except twelve men that Joshua had instructed to stay on the other side.

Why had Joshua commanded them to stay?

Joshua said to them, "See where the priests are standing; there are great stones lying near them. Take up twelve great stones and bring them over with you into Canaan." These twelve men walked through the dry path. Each took up a great stone in his arms and carried it to the other side. Then Joshua said to them, "Put the twelve stones by the side of the river in Canaan."

Why do you think the stones were to be put there?

It was that people might never forget this great wonder of making a path in Jordan. God knew that, a long time afterwards, little children would see the twelve stones and would say to their fathers, "What are these stones for?"

Then their fathers would say, "These stones were once at the bottom of the water but God made a path for us and we have put the stones here to keep God's kindness in our minds."

God is pleased that children would wish to know the meaning of what they see. God wishes little children to know about his goodness and the wonders that he has done.

All the time the twelve men were walking through with the stones the priests were standing still in the river.

At last Joshua said to the priests, "Come up out of Jordan" so the priests came up out of the river. As soon as the priests put their feet on the dry land in Canaan the water rolled along and the river looked as it had done before.

How happy the Israelites must now have been! They had wandered forty years in the wilderness but at last they had safely arrived in Canaan. God had been very good to them and he would help them fight against the wicked people of Canaan.

Why did God want the people in Canaan to be killed? Because they went on worshipping idols and doing many wicked things so God chose to punish them.

The king of Jericho saw the Israelites come over the river. He could look at them over his high walls. He was very much frightened and so were all the people in Jericho. Only Rahab was not frightened. She knew she was safe - she believed in the true God.

The priests put down the ark. All the Israelites set up their tents and waited outside Jericho. Rahab's red cord could be seen upon her window on the wall.

So the Israelites knew which was her house and Joshua told them not to hurt the people who were in it.

The gates of Jericho were closed so that the Israelites might not get in. No one in Jericho went out and no one came in but everybody kept inside the town.

Those wicked people would never again walk by the riverside. The day of their death was very near. Ah! Why did they not turn to God before it was too late?

The day of judgment will come to us at last. Now is the time to be sorry for our sins and to ask God for his Holy Spirit. If children will go on telling lies, quarrelling, fighting, being bold and disobedient, they will come to a sad end.

But I hope that you will love God and that you will be saved.

Questions for Chapter 37

What would the Israelites have to cross before they could get into Canaan?

What did Joshua desire the priests to do?

What happened when the priests put their feet into the river Jordan?

Where did the priests stop while the people were crossing the river?

Why did Joshua desire twelve men to take up twelve stones from the river and to place them in Canaan?

When did the water of the river cover up the dry path again?

How long had the Israelites been travelling through the wilderness?

Who were the only persons in Jericho whom God meant to save?

Why did God desire the Israelites to kill the other people in Jericho?

Scripture Verse

When we ought to seek for mercy from God.
'Seek ye the Lord while he may be found, call ye upon him while he is near.' - (Isa. 55:6).

Notes for Chapter 37

1. In the passage of the Jordan the waters stood up on *one* side only, not, as in the passage of the Red Sea, on *both* sides. God stopped the waters that were flowing towards the Dead Sea and made those waters stand in a heap while all below the heap, as far as the Dead Sea, was dried up - (See Joshua 3:16).

CHAPTER 38
JOSHUA AND THE WALLS OF JERICHO
Josh. 5:13-15; 6.

The children of Israel had placed their tents all round the city of Jericho but they waited till God told them what to do. They could not get through the strong gates unless God helped them.

Joshua was the captain of the Israelites. He was a very brave man. He trusted God to help him and that made him brave. I will now tell you a very wonderful thing that happened to Joshua while he was on the outside of Jericho.

One day he looked up and he saw a man standing before him a little way off. The man looked as if he was a soldier and he held a sword in his hand. Joshua knew that this man was not one of the Israelites but he could not tell who he was.

Joshua went up to the man and said, "Have you come to help us to fight? Or have you come to help the people of Jericho?"

Then the man answered, "I have come as captain of the army of the Lord."

Now Joshua knew who this man was. Can you tell me who he was?

He was greater than a man, greater than an angel. He was the Lord from heaven, Jesus Christ.

Jesus did not become a little baby for a long time afterwards but he always lived in heaven with his Father and sometimes looked like a man and came down upon the earth.[1]

Was it not very kind of the Lord Jesus to come down from heaven and speak to Joshua?

When Joshua knew who the man was, he fell down with his face upon the ground and worshipped him saying, "What will my Lord say to his servant?"(Joshua called himself God's servant.)

Then the great captain of God's army said, "Take your shoe off your foot because this is holy ground."

Then Joshua took it off and waited to know what the Lord would say to him. Why was the ground holy? Because God was there. You know the priests wore no shoes when they walked in God's house.

The Lord told Joshua how he was to fight against Jericho. Such a way of fighting was never known before. You shall soon hear what the Lord told Joshua to do.

When the commander had gone back to heaven Joshua called the priests and all the people of Israel and showed them what they must do. Joshua told some of the priests to take up the ark. Then he called seven more priests and said, "Each of you must take a trumpet[2] and walk before the ark."

Then Joshua called all the soldiers and told them to go before the priests and he told the rest of the people that did not have swords or spears (that is, the women and children) to walk behind the priests.

Where were they all to walk? Joshua commanded them to walk round the city of Jericho. The soldiers with their swords and spears went first. Next came seven priests dressed in their white clothes, blowing the trumpets. Then came the priests carrying the ark and behind them all the people but with no swords or spears. You never saw such a great number of people walking along.

Before they set out, Joshua told them not to start shouting but to wait till he said, "Shout!"

What is shouting? Calling out loud. Soldiers shout when they have conquered. The Israelites were not to shout till Joshua told them. They all walked once round Jericho. The people of Jericho heard the trumpets blowing and they saw the men with swords and spears.

I dare say they thought the Israelites were going to shoot their arrows over the walls and try and beat down the walls. How frightened they must have been! Rahab took care to stay in her house with all her dear friends. The Israelites walked once round and then Joshua brought them back to their tents.

Are you not surprised to hear this? What was the use of walking round? You will hear what happened in the end.

The next day Joshua made the people and the priests walk round once more and then brought them home. Then, the day after they went round again and the next day and the next day. Six days, one after the other, they walked round Jericho and came home to their tents again without having fought.

The Israelites behaved well in doing as Joshua told them instead of asking why they must walk round without fighting.

Do you think that the people of Jericho began to laugh at the Israelites and to think that they never would get into the city?

At last, after six days, Joshua told the Israelites to get up very early in the morning, as soon as it was light. He told them to walk all round as before but when they had walked round he did not tell them to go back to their tents but to walk round again. That day they walked round seven times. They spent the whole day in walking round and round the city of Jericho.

When they had just finished walking round the seventh time Joshua said to the people, "Now, when the priests blow again with the trumpets, you may shout because God has given you the city. You will soon get in. You must kill all the people, except Rahab and her friends who are in her house. You will find many beautiful things in Jericho but you must not keep anything for yourselves. You must bring the cups of gold and silver and brass and iron to the Lord. You must not keep anything for yourselves. Bring all you find to the house of the Lord because God has cursed Jericho and everything in it."

When Joshua had finished speaking the priests blew again with the trumpets and the people gave a great shout. At the same moment the walls of Jericho fell down. How horrible was the crash of those great walls! Now the men of Jericho saw that the day was come when they must die.

The two spies ran quickly to Rahab's house and brought her out and her father and mother, brothers and sisters and led them to a safe place near the tents of the Israelites. Rahab and her friends brought all their things with them out of the house so they could make tents and live together. O happy Rahab! Now she could learn more about the true God. She could see God's priests offering sacrifices on the altar and could hear how her sins might be forgiven by the blood of Jesus, the Lamb of God, who would come into the world.

But what happened to the people of Jericho? They were all killed, the men, the women and the children. Even the sheep and cows and all the animals were killed; not one was left alive. The Israelites killed them with their swords. Then they set fire to the houses and burned them all up but the cups and basins, made of gold and silver and brass and iron, they brought to the priests for God's house. What would the priests do with the basins? They would put in them the blood of sheep and goats that they sacrificed on the altar.

All the other people in Canaan heard about Jericho and they were more frightened than before. They said, "What a great captain Joshua is!"

But you know who was the Captain that fought for Joshua. Who was it that broke down the walls? Was it not the man whom Joshua had seen? He was a captain over thousands of angels that filled the air and obeyed all he said. The angels are stronger than men. Jesus is their captain and he is God himself. He can break down walls and he can build them up. He can kill and he can make alive. He can shut us up in hell and he can lift us up to heaven. Which do you wish him to do for you? Let us pray to him to save us when the world is burnt up; as he saved Rahab when Jericho was burnt up.

Questions for Chapter 38

Who was the man with the sword that Joshua saw near Jericho?
Who told Joshua how to conquer Jericho?
Who was to blow the rams' horns?
How many days did the Israelites walk round Jericho?
How many times did they walk round on the seventh day?
What did the *people* do *just* before the walls fell down?
What did the *priests* do *just* before the walls fell down?
What became of the people of Jericho?
What became of the city of Jericho?
What day does the burning of Jericho make you think of?

Scripture Verse

What shall become at last of the wicked.
'Let the sinners be consumed out of the earth and let the wicked be no more...' - (Ps. 104:35).

Notes for Chapter 38

[1] Dan. 3:25; Mic. 5:2.
[2] The word translated ram's horn is thought to refer to the silver trumpets.

CHAPTER 39
THE DEATH OF JOSHUA

You have heard what the Israelites did to Jericho. There were many other cities in Canaan besides Jericho. The Israelites fought against the other cities of Canaan.

All the people in Canaan heard of it and were very afraid of Joshua but still they took their swords and spears and fought against them.

And who do you think conquered? God always helped the Israelites so they always conquered. They went all through Canaan. First, they went to one city and killed the people in it; then they went to another city and killed the people in it so they went to hundreds of cities till they had killed almost all the people in Canaan. God did not make the walls of the other cities fall down, like the walls of Jericho, but the Israelites were obliged to fight very hard before they could get in.

At last, Joshua said to the children of Israel, "Now the people of Canaan are dead. I will give you places to live in." So he gave to each of the Israelites a house, full of beautiful things and a garden, a field and a well of water.

Now the Israelites rested. They sat down under the fig trees and vines in their own gardens and ate the figs and grapes that grew on them and they drank water out of the wells in their gardens.

Did the Israelites build their own houses? No, they lived in the houses of the people of Canaan. The wicked people had built the houses, they had dug the wells and planted the trees in the gardens[1] but God had taken them away from these wicked people and had given them to the Israelites.

Can God give them to whom He pleases? Yes, God made everything and everything belongs to God. He may give things to whom he pleases. Sometimes he takes his things away from wicked people.

When the Israelites sat in their gardens they ought to have thought to themselves, "How kind of God to give us so much! How much we ought to love him!"

Has not God given you many things? Should you love God very much?

Why did God give so many things to the Israelites? Were the Israelites good? No, they were naughty. Then why was God so kind to them?

You remember the promise God had made to Abraham. God had said that he would give Canaan to his children's children. And did God keep his word? O, yes! He remembered his promise and he brought the Israelites into Canaan.[2] So the reason God was so kind to the Israelites was, because he had promised Abraham he would be kind to his children.

There was one thing which Joshua did not forget to do, that was, to place the tabernacle in Canaan. He set it up in the middle of Canaan at a place called Shiloh. Now the Israelites would not be obliged to move it about any more.

Joshua told them all to come up and worship God in the tabernacle but some lived so far off that they could not come often. So they came only sometimes to the tabernacle.

God commanded the Israelites not to worship the idols that the wicked people in Canaan had made. The Israelites would find their idols in the fields and gardens. Some of their idols were made of silver and gold but the Israelites were not to keep them. Even if they were pretty images they were not to take the idols into their houses but they were to burn them in the fire because God hated these idols.[3]

At last Joshua grew very old and he knew that he must die. So he called many of the Israelites together that he might speak to them before he died.

Joshua stood near a great oak tree while he spoke. He said to the Israelites, "I am soon going to die. Whom will you worship after I am dead? Will you worship idols or will you worship God who has been so kind to you?"

Now which do you think the Israelites would choose to worship? They all said, "We will worship God."

Then Joshua said, "If you choose to worship God you must not worship idols too."

Then they answered, "We will serve God."

"Now," said Joshua, "you have promised to serve God only. You must keep your promise.

Then Joshua took a book and wrote down what the people had said. Afterwards Joshua took a great stone and put it under the oak and said, "See this stone; I have put it here to make you remember your promise always."

Then Joshua told all the people to go home.

Very soon afterwards Joshua died. He was more than a hundred years old when he died.

Did the Israelites keep their promise? Did they worship idols, or did they not?

At first they did not worship idols. But at last they grew tired of serving God and began to worship idols and to do other wicked things.

Your parents have not taught you to worship idols but you have done other naughty things. Have you never been disobedient, nor told lies, nor lost your temper?

What can you do to please God?[4] Speak the truth, obey your parents and be very kind to each other. These are things that please God.

Do you wish to please God who has been kind to you and has given you food, clothes, a house, kind friends, a body and a soul and who has even given his Son to die for you? Ask God to make you love him and wish to please him.

Questions for Chapter 39

What did Joshua give to the Israelites after the people in Canaan were all killed?

Why did God give so much to the Israelites?

Why did God desire the Israelites to kill the people in Canaan?

Where did Joshua place the tabernacle?

What had God commanded the Israelites to do with the wicked people's idols?

What question did Joshua ask the Israelites before he died?

What promise did the Israelites make to Joshua?

Why did Joshua place a stone under the oak tree?

Why ought we to love God and to try and please him?

Scripture Verse

Praise to God for His goodness.

'Bless the Lord, O my soul and forget not all his benefits; who forgiveth all thine iniquities, who healeth all thy diseases.' - (Ps. 103:2,3).

Notes for Chapter 39

[1] Deut. 6:10,11.   [2] Deut. 6:10.   [3] Deut. 7:25,26.
[4] 1 Thess 4:1.

QUESTIONS FOR THOSE WHO HAVE COMPLETED THE BOOK

1. What promise did the Lord Jesus make to his Father a long time before Adam and Eve had sinned?

2. How did the people offer sacrifices?

3. Why did God want people to offer sacrifices?

4. Why did Cain kill Abel?

5. Why did God drown the world?

6. Whom did God save when the world was drowned?

7. Whom did God want to leave his own country and to go to a land that he would show him?

8. What land did God promise to give to Abraham's children's children?

9. What was the name of Abraham's son?

10. What were the names of Isaac's two sons?

11. How many sons had Jacob?

12. What cruel thing did Joseph's brothers do to him?

13. Why did the king of Egypt make Joseph a great lord?

14. How did Joseph save people from starving when scarcely any corn grew in the fields?

15. Where did Joseph ask his brothers to come and live?

16. What was Jacob's name?

17. Who were the Israelites?

18. Who wanted the babies of the Israelites to be drowned?

19. Who found Moses in the river and called him her son?

20. When Moses was grown up where did he wish to take the Israelites?

21. Where did God command Moses to go when he spoke to him in the burning bush?

22. Why did God send ten plagues to king Pharaoh?

23. On the night that the eldest sons were killed, what did the Israelites eat and what did they sprinkle on their doors.

24. What was the name of that supper?

25. How were Pharaoh and his servants killed?

26. How did the Israelites know which way to go to Canaan?

27. How were they fed in the wilderness?

28. What words did God speak very loudly from Mount Sinai?

29. When Moses was alone with God on Mount Sinai what did God command him to make?

30. Who was to be the high priest?

31. What was the ark of God?

32. Why did the Israelites send twelve spies into Canaan?

33. Why did the Israelites say they would go back into Egypt?

34. What punishment did God give the Israelites for murmuring at what the spies had said?

35. Why ought the Israelites not to have been afraid of the strong men in Canaan?

36. How did Moses and Aaron offend God?

37. Whom did God desire to take care of the Israelites after Moses was dead?

38. What was the first city in Canaan that the Israelites conquered?

39. Why did God bring the Israelites into Canaan?

40. Why did God desire the Israelites to kill the people of Canaan?

<u>NOTES</u>

<u>NOTES</u>

NOTES

<u>NOTES</u>

NOTES

<u>NOTES</u>

<u>NOTES</u>

<u>NOTES</u>

NOTES

<u>NOTES</u>

<u>NOTES</u>

<u>NOTES</u>

<u>NOTES</u>

CHRISTIAN FOCUS

Good books with the real message of hope!

Christian Focus Publications publishes
biblically-accurate books for adults and children.

If you are looking for quality Bible teaching for
children then we have a wide and excellent range
of Bible story books - from board books to
teenage fiction, we have it covered.

 You can also try our new Bible teaching
Syllabus for 3-9 year olds and teaching materials
for pre-school children.

 These children's books are bright, fun and
full of biblical truth, an ideal way to help children
discover Jesus Christ for themselves. Our aim
is to help children find out about God and get
them enthusiastic about reading the Bible, now
and later in their life.

Find us at our web page: www.christianfocus.com